HIP TASTES

HIP TASTES

The Fresh Guide to Wine

COURTNEY COCHRAN

Illustrations by
Donna Mehalko

Viking Studio

VIKING STUDIO
Published by the Penguin Group
Penguin Group (USA) Inc., 375 Hudson Street, New York, New York 10014, U.S.A.
Penguin Group (Canada), 90 Eglinton Avenue East, Suite 700, Toronto, Ontario, Canada
M4P 2Y3 (a division of Pearson Penguin Canada Inc.)
Penguin Books Ltd, 80 Strand, London WC2R 0RL, England
Penguin Ireland, 25 St. Stephen's Green, Dublin 2, Ireland (a division of Penguin Books Ltd)
Penguin Books Australia Ltd, 250 Camberwell Road, Camberwell, Victoria 3124,
Australia (a division of Pearson Australia Group Pty Ltd)
Penguin Books India Pvt Ltd, 11 Community Centre, Panchsheel Park,
New Delhi–110 017, India
Penguin Group (NZ), 67 Apollo Drive, Rosedale, North Shore 0632,
New Zealand (a division of Pearson New Zealand Ltd)
Penguin Books (South Africa) (Pty) Ltd, 24 Sturdee Avenue, Rosebank, Johannesburg
2196, South Africa

Penguin Books Ltd, Registered Offices: 80 Strand, London WC2R 0RL, England

First published in 2007 by Viking Studio, a member of Penguin Group (USA) Inc.

10 9 8 7 6 5 4 3 2 1

Copyright © Courtney Cochran, 2007
All rights reserved

Illustrations by Donna Mehalko

Your Personal Sommelier and Hip Tastes are registered trademarks of Courtney Cochran.

LIBRARY OF CONGRESS CATALOGING-IN-PUBLICATION DATA
Cochran, Courtney.
Hip tastes : the fresh guide to wine / Courtney Cochran ; illustrations by Donna Mehalko.
p.   cm.
Includes index.
ISBN 978-0-14-200519-4
1. Wine and wine making—Guidebooks.   2. Wine and wine making—Amateurs'
manuals.   I. Mehalko, Donna.   II. Title.
TP548.2.C63 2007
641.2'2—dc22   2007014681

Printed in the United States of America
Set in Bembo
Designed by Spring Hoteling

For my sister Claire, the original hip taster

Contents

There's never been a better time to learn about wine. Across the land, wineshops, bars, and tasting groups are springing up faster than Internet start-ups in 1999. You'd like to get in on the action, but—up until now—haven't found a fun, relatable resource to help you get started.

Welcome to *Hip Tastes: The Fresh Guide to Wine*. If you're picking up this book because you'd like to learn more about wine quickly, painlessly, and with a refreshing dash of humor and style, you're off to a great start. *Hip Tastes* packages practical wine knowledge that every budding enthusiast should know in a fresh format that brings wine out of the realm of stuffy critics and stodgy wine snobs and back down to earth, where it ought to be.

It's Time to Get in on the Action!

In ten easy-to-digest chapters you'll learn how to sip wine like a pro, pair wines with food, order nimbly in restaurants, and throw fabulous wine tastings in your own home, among other fun tricks. Each topic is presented in detail alongside practical supporting information such as reliable producers, appropriate service temperatures, and bargain alternatives. So you can get back to your fabulous life, but know when to pick a Cava over a Prosecco and when a certain Sicilian red is just the thing to pacify your overbearing boss.

Who Am I?

I'm just a regular gal who, armed with my newly minted MBA and sommelier certification, segued from an otherwise completely normal career path into what I'm doing now. Which is, essentially, tasting and writing about wine for a living. That, and I also throw stylish monthly wine parties for adventurous enthusiasts through my San Francisco–based special-events company, HIP TASTES Events—the inspiration for this book!

During my short career as a so-called wine expert I've been profiled in the media and have worked as a private sommelier for employees at tony institutions like Deloitte & Touche and IBM. It all feels too wonderfully fabulous to be true, and I keep waiting for someone to tell me, *Thank you, but the show's over, and it's time to return to the real world.* Happily, no one has, so I keep on doing my thing!

And now, I couldn't be more pleased to be bringing the spirit and enthusiasm of HIP TASTES Events to hip tasters all over the country with the *Hip Tastes* book. I hope you enjoy it, I hope you learn a lot, and I hope you view it as the beginning of a great journey you're taking. Because one thing I've learned when it comes to wine is that you never stop learning. Or, as the HIP TASTES Events tagline reminds us: *You can never get enough of the good stuff.*

How to Use This Book

You have a job. You have responsibilities. In short, you have a life.

As much as I'd like to picture you spending umpteen hours poring over this book, I know the reality is that we all have other important things to do besides learning how to become the next Tiger Woods of wine. That's why I devised *Hip Tastes* to deliver the key, really critical facts about wine quickly and memorably, so you can take it all in and then get straight to the good part: putting it to use in the real world.

Your CliffsNotes to the Wine World

The first chapter is called, fittingly, "A Crash Course: Your CliffsNotes to the Wine World," and includes what I've found during my own wine studies and on the job to be the most essential information for forming a good foundation in wine. In it you'll find up-to-date, concise information on everything from the history of winemaking and the key wine regions of the world to major wine styles and wine-naming rationales.

Once you've finished Chapter 1, the other chapters build upon the knowledge you've developed. In Chapter 2 you'll learn how to taste wine like a pro (and impress your friends/family/coworkers with your newfound skills!), and in Chapters 3 and 4 you'll learn about the major grape varieties of the world and their characteristics, so you can really mean it when you insist that no, thank you, you really prefer a Cab to a Pinot.

Chapter 5 will bring you up to speed on some of the other major styles of wine out there—bubblies and sweet wines—before Chapter 6 breaks down the mysterious world of wine and food pairing (clue: It's actually not that tough but requires mastery of a few key rules). Other topics covered include entertaining with wine, shopping for the good stuff, and wine travel.

And when you're through with all that, you can comb through the Appendix to find lots of to-the-point tips on all sorts of other useful wine wisdom, at your leisure.

And You're Off!

In all, it's a whirlwind education in wine—which is exactly how I'd want it to be if I was back at the beginning of my own wine journey. Because, at the end of the day, the best part of learning about wine is putting your newfound skills to use. And the sooner you wrap *Hip Tastes,* the sooner you can do just that.

HIP TASTES

Fish out of Water

I showed up for the first day of my sommelier training course lugging the five textbooks listed as required reading for the class. As I lurched through the door, nearly toppling under the load, I caught sight of my classmates: Not one of them had brought the books to class.

Most of them were employed waiting tables, tending bar, or, in some instances, already running wine programs at upscale Los Angeles eateries. At the time, I was in graduate school at UCLA studying for my master's in business administration, and was the sole "businessperson" in the course. Accustomed to lugging accounting and economics textbooks to my classes at UCLA, I'd assumed I would need an arsenal of textbooks for wine class, too.

Boy, was I wrong.

I quickly learned from my classmates that, more than anything, learning about wine comes from the experience of drinking it. Textbook learning, although helpful in lending color to what we were absorbing along the way, is really more of a supporting act when it comes to grasping the essence of the good stuff. And so, in this spirit, I've condensed the highlights of all those books into just one resource, *Hip Tastes,* which is why I encourage you to use *this* book as a backdrop for your own wine education. Reading it will bring you quickly up to speed on the fundamentals, but you won't need to pore over it for hours with highlighter poised, as you would with a pesky textbook. So, lose the highlighter and—*please!*—toss aside that notepad and pen. Instead, pour yourself a nice glass of wine, put your feet up, and get ready to take your wine IQ to the next level.

Chapter 1

A Crash Course
Your CliffsNotes to the Wine World

All right, folks, fasten your seat belts.

I'm going to jump right into the thick of things here, covering everything from the history of wine to how it's made to how to tell a good bottle from something you wouldn't serve your worst enemy. I'll also tackle the major wine regions and key styles, as well as the rationale behind how wines are named. If I do my job, this chapter will give you the foundation you need to become a fabulously informed hip taster in no time.

First, a Brief History Lesson

For just about as long as people have been gathering in groups resembling what your fourth-grade history teacher earnestly dubbed a "civilization," they've been making wine. Meaning, folks discovered really fast way back when that you can make alcohol from fermenting the sugar found in just about any sort of raw plant material, including, of course, grapes. More on this later.

Wine first made its debut on the global history scene with the Mesopotamians around 6000 BC, when these savvy trailblazers grew the first documented grapevines. The Greeks later honed the process of grape growing and winemaking, but it wasn't until the era of the Romans that things got seriously under way on the wine scene. As the ambitious Romans spread their empire throughout modern-day Europe and beyond, they brought with them a budding grape-growing and winemaking culture that took root, literally, pretty much wherever they went. In fact, many of Europe's most famous wine-growing regions were established way back then, and have changed little since. You've got to give the Romans credit—they were onto something good!

Things have been pretty much onward and upward ever since the Romans gave the wine movement that catalyzing kick in the pants. And, as anyone who's enjoyed a California Pinot or a South African Pinotage can attest, wine is now grown not only in Europe but in all parts of the world where the climate's suitable. Today, in fact, nearly eight billion gallons of wine are produced annually around the world, testament to the remarkable appeal of the stuff in modern times.

Making It Happen: From Vine to Wine

Now, for the critical question: Just how exactly is wine made, anyway? You may recall from earlier that it's got something to do with the fermentation of plant sugar into alcohol. That's essentially it, but there are a few other things that have to happen along the way to produce really outstanding vino. Let's take a look at just what those things are for top-quality wine production.

No Junk Food!

First off, I'd like to debunk the myth that great wine is made in the winery. *Au contraire!* Really excellent, top stuff—the kind of stuff that I like to write about and the reason I'm in this industry to begin with—couldn't be made if the vines didn't first receive outstanding care and attention in the vineyard. The most conscientious growers, in fact, avoid using chemical fertilizers or other additives— something a wise sommelier once appropriately dubbed "junk food for grapes"—whenever possible, as these dilute the quality of the fruit and ultimately result in bland-tasting wine that's indistinguishable from one bottle to the next.

Which is a pity, because wine should really be about personality.

Just as an organically grown strawberry may be smaller in size but much more flavorful than its industrially pro-duced, hormone-jacked counterpart, wine grapes grown with minimal chemical interference produce the most lay-ered and interesting wines, with the best clarity of flavor.

All About Organics

Organic wine is a hot—if often misunderstood— topic. There are two key ways in which a wine can be organic:

- The raw material is organic. Wines made from organically grown grapes—from vine-yards that are "certified organic"—may be indicated on the label.
- The raw material is organic *and* the wine has been made organically. These wines are con-sidered truly organic by the U.S. Department

of Agriculture. Not only are the grapes raised in certified organic vineyards, the wine has been made without the use of added sulfites (sulfur dioxide). And although many wines still contain naturally occuring sulfites, the level may not surpass 100 parts per million in organic wines.

While many growers are embracing organic farming, few winemakers have opted to follow the more restrictive route required for their wines to be considered truly organic. This is because sulfur dioxide is a preservative that many believe essential to a wine's longevity and durability during shipping, thanks to its antimicrobial and antioxidant properties. However, some consumers' sensitivity to sulfites has in part fueled the movement toward decreasing their use in winemaking. Expect the debate—and the confusion—to continue!

To learn more about organic wine, visit the Web site organicconsumers.org.

Ter-*what?*

Which brings up another important point when it comes to growing wine grapes (technically speaking, "viticulture" or "vineyard management"). The French word *terroir* is much tossed about among the wine cognoscenti, and for very good reasons. Unlike so many other contrived and snotty-sounding wine terms, this is one that I absolutely, unapologetically, get behind.

Terroir refers to everything that happens around a grapevine during the course of its life. This includes the composition of the soil underneath it, the degree of slope on which it's planted, the surrounding climate, and its genetic makeup. Because different grapes (e.g., Chardonnay versus

Sauvignon Blanc) possess their own optimal combinations of all of these factors, it's critically important that you've got the right vine planted in its particular plot! As a point of reference, people are a lot like this, too: Pacific North-westerners, for example, are accustomed to the rainy weather found in Seattle, but the constant precipitation there would likely send a Texan skedaddling for the in-doors, if not for the next flight home. (Easy, Texans! It's just a hypothetical.)

I'll go into greater detail on different grape varieties and where they're most happy in terms of location in Chapters 3 and 4. For now, though, let's take a closer look at the other building blocks of this *terroir* thing.

Soil—the Worse, the Better

One of the most puzzling rules of thumb in the wine world is that the best wine comes from vines planted in the worst (read: poorest) soil. Confusing though it may sound at first, the poorest soils when it comes to grapevines—and therefore the best, really—are those that possess a layer of thin, well-drained topsoil on top of complex, mineral-laced stuff down below. Unlike corn, cabbage, and most other commercial crops, grapevines are at their best when they have to really struggle to reach the nutrients they need to produce their fruit.

This struggle—which I like to call the "good struggle"— causes the vines to absorb all sorts of interesting elements from the soil along their journey underground. These ele-ments, in turn, impart nuance and character—personality— to the finished wine. The longer a vine is allowed to mature, the farther it will extend its roots into the ground, the more nutrients it will pick up along the way, and the more personality its wine will possess. It bears noting, however, that this is true up to a certain point. Grapevines produce less and less fruit as they age and tend to peter out after about fifty years, when they no longer produce enough fruit to be economically viable. Some producers continue to harvest minuscule amounts of fruit from older vines, as this fruit has the greatest concentration—but these wines are correspondingly expensive.

Good drainage is critical as well, so that the roots extending deep into the ground are able to get the vital water they need to survive. This is why some of the most famous vineyards in the world are literally covered in rocks. There's nothing better for drainage! By the same token, vines grown in mountainous soil—which tends to have the poorest topsoil and the richest treasure trove of minerals underneath—make some of the world's most fascinating and multidimensional wines. Another way to look at it is: Plant vines in so-called "healthy" soil and expect boring wine.

Exposure—Not Too Little, Never Too Much

Vines love an open hill.
—the Roman poet Virgil, on the subject of exposure

Grapevines, like all plants, need sunshine to thrive. And as with other plant life, give them too much and they wither, too little and they never get off the ground. This is where exposure, or the situation of a grapevine in relation to the sun, comes into play.

It's vitally important that wine grapes receive adequate sunshine hours to ripen fully, but they're also intolerant of constantly scorching heat. Notice we're not talking about growing grapes along the sun-baked equator—it's way too hot there for the vines to function. Instead, vines situated on hillsides within the wine-friendly regions of the globe (more on this later) benefit from the longest hours of exposure to the warming rays of the sun without getting overheated.

This ideal combination of mild temperature and abundant sunshine allows grapes to develop both the rich flavors we look for in a satisfying glass of wine and the core of mouthwatering acidity that makes it the perfect partner for food. And remember mountain wines? They've *really* got it going on: poor soil *and* hillside sites for optimum sun exposure. Beginning to see a trend?

> ## High Altitude "Hot Spots"
>
> Mendoza, Argentina
> Meknes, Morocco
> Douro Valley, Portugal
> Alto Adige, Italy
> Santa Cruz Mountains, California

Climate and Weather—Key Players

Possibly the most important components of the *terroir* equation, weather and climate are responsible for a vine's producing palatable wine one year and then rancid, undrinkable stuff the next. They're often to blame when a wine is too tart (too cold!) as well as too "flabby," or lacking in acid (not cold enough!). But an ideal growing climate and hospitable weather can facilitate the production of superlative, utterly memorable, and fabulously layered wine.

Vitis vinifera, the grapevine species we can thank for giving us wine, is only able to thrive between about 30° and 50° latitude north and south of the equator, in areas where the average annual temperature clocks in somewhere between 50° and 68° Fahrenheit. To give you an idea of what this band of what I like to call "wine-friendly" territory encompasses in our own little slice of the northern hemisphere, it's roughly north of the Baja Peninsula (think Mexico's Ensenada) on the West Coast and Miami's South Beach on the East, and south of Canada's Vancouver (yeah, Whistler!) in the west and Quebec in the east.

You don't have to be a genius to note that this area includes just about all of the United States! But surely you've also noticed that grapevines don't cover every cultivable inch of land we've got. It's quite the opposite, actually: *Vinifera* vines are grown on only about 0.04 percent of this country's total land area. This is because once a vine finds itself inside our band of so-called wine-friendly territory, other factors must be in place in order for it to succeed and thrive here. The first is consistency of temperature: Wine grapes require a nice long, warm, and mostly dry growing season (in the Northern Hemisphere, that's from mid-March to mid-October) in order to bear fruit. This narrows things down quite a bit in terms of places that fit the bill. California, with its mostly dry, balmy weather, is home to the lion's share of U.S. vineyards—approximately 95 percent of U.S. wine exports come from the Golden State.

And as I mentioned before, grapevines like warmth but they can't bear constant heat. This is why the best areas for grape growing are those situated near some kind of cooling influence, often a nearby body of water. Along the hot California coast, for example, cooling relief takes the form of the late afternoon fog that rolls in off the Pacific and cools down the grapes in the early evening hours. Water's mitigating role works the other way, too: Cooler regions such as British Columbia's Okanagan Valley can grow vines successfully, but in these instances the naturally *cool* temperatures there are offset in the *other direction*—warmed up—by the presence of a nearby body of water. And, coming back to mountain wines, altitude plays a key role in that climatic scenario as well. Altitude, like water, has a critical influence on vines, as those planted at higher elevations in warm areas—even areas that are otherwise too hot to grow vines—are able to thrive, because the average temperature tends to be cooler higher up.

Hip Facts

Fitting name for a wine vine: Vinifera literally means "wine bearing."

Cool slopes: Every 500 feet above sea level the temperature drops about 3° Fahrenheit.

Totally tartaric: Tartaric acid lends white wines their lip-smackingly tart flavor.

Viticulture—Vine Care 411

So now that we know that the best wines are really made in the vineyard, let's take a closer look at what that means. The best vineyards have all the parts of the *terroir* equation in lockstep, but it's also critical that the grapes are harvested at the optimal time. Grapes begin to ripen fully as summer winds down (around Labor Day in the Northern Hemisphere) and, depending on the particular grape variety in question, harvest begins at that time and continues over the next couple of months, usually winding down by Halloween. Generally speaking, the whites are harvested first and the reds later, although there is some overlap.

The real trick to harvesting is timing. Weather is always a concern, with early autumn rains the main culprit in ruining an otherwise perfectly good crop. On the other hand, you don't want to pick too early, because the grapes won't be at their optimal ripeness. Growers tell me all the time that they're on pins and needles throughout the harvest season, until the last bunch of grapes comes in. When that happens, as you might imagine, they usually heave a big sigh of relief and celebrate—if they have any energy left!

Besides the harvest-timing issue, fruit from the best

vineyards is always handled with kid gloves. This usually means harvesting exclusively by hand, and then hand sorting the clusters to weed out any subpar fruit. This is the wine equivalent of VIP treatment. Alternatives include mechanical harvesting and machine sorting, which are not necessarily bad techniques, although they afford less precision in terms of ferreting out the best fruit. However it's done, after all the grapes are picked it's time for the winemaker to step into the spotlight and take over the operation.

In other words, it's time to make some wine!

Fermentation—How the Good Stuff's Made

The same initial process is used to make both jug wine and Domaine de la Romanée-Conti—the world's most expensive Pinot Noir—with a couple of notable adjustments down the line for the latter.

Let's talk about the fundamental first step, which is the same for both the jug wine and the Romanée-Conti, and all other wines for that matter. Fermentation is a chemical process that converts the sugars naturally found in all sorts of plants—including potatoes, grains, and yep, grapes—into alcohol. The key factor in jump-starting the process is the presence of airborne yeasts that catalyze the conversion of the sugar into alcohol. When it comes to winemaking, the yeasts used can be naturally occuring in the air around the grape "must"—or juice—or they can be of the "bag o' yeast" variety, which are essentially artificially cultivated yeasts that are added to the fermentation vessel by the winemaker at just the right time. Using artificial yeasts allows winemakers to control the timing of fermentation more precisely, although some folks, including yours truly, find wines made with naturally occuring yeasts a bit more interesting.

Pasteur Would Be Proud!

Yeast makes wine, bacteria destroy it.
—Louis Pasteur

Fab Frenchman Louis Pasteur's discovery that microorganisms trigger wine spoilage led to his groundbreaking discoveries that help prevent diseases in humans.

The sugar in the grapes is eventually "eaten up" by the yeast until the sugar is entirely converted into alcohol. As we like to say in the wine business, the stuff at this point has been "fermented to dryness." This is why most wines are, by definition, dry—meaning that they literally have little or no residual sugar left in them by the time they're bottled. If you think you're tasting something "sweet" when you taste a wine, it's highly likely you're just tasting ripe fruit flavors that *seem* sweet. Technically, however, most wines are dry, baby, dry!

Raising and Bottling—Pulling It All Together

Fermentation usually takes a couple of weeks to run its course, after which the winemaker will transfer the wine from the fermentation tank into another container, where it will stay for an amount of time suitable to the kind of wine it's destined to be. Whites and reds *not* destined for oak aging will be transferred into steel, concrete, or tile-lined vats to harmonize and integrate for several months prior to bottling. Rich reds and whites meant for oak maturation will, on the other hand, be transferred to oak barrels or large oak casks to continue their development, sometimes for years.

:::

The Lowdown on Nouveau Wines

The Nouveau wines from France's famous Beaujolais region are released just weeks after the grapes
are picked, as soon as fermentation stops and the
stuff can be bottled. Sometimes called "early bird
wines," Beaujolais Nouveau reds are fresh, fruity
wines meant to be enjoyed young with bistro fare
and other simple foods. Millions of gallons of the
stuff are sold every fall worldwide.

:::

When the time finally comes for bottling, the wine will
be moved from its container into bottles and labeled, after
which it will be either shipped to retail shelves for consumption by folks like you and me, or sent back into storage for further development—sometimes for several or
more years—before it's released for sale. In fact, some wine
regions, such as Spain's Rioja and Portugal's Douro, where
they make port, impose mandatory waiting periods before
some bottled wines can be released. This is generally a good
thing, as the wines develop still more nuance and character
during this extra time of "bottle aging," as it's called.

Wine Styles

Generally speaking, there are three key things that determine a wine's style:

- Grape variety
- Climate
- Winemaking technique

Grape Variety

Grape varieties, which I'll profile in detail in Chapters 3
and 4, are what you might call the dominant factors in

determining a wine's style. They determine in the broadest sense what kind of wine you're going to have: light and crisp (Sauvignon Blanc), full and lush (Viognier), spicy and rich (Zinfandel), or smooth and earthy (Pinot Noir). Once the grape variety sets the tone for the wine, the other key factors in the style equation—climate and winemaking technique—lend nuance and detail to the picture.

Climate

Climate, as we know from earlier, has a strong influence on a wine's personality. For example, Sauvignon Blanc from balmy California tends to be rather rich for this usually lean grape, with heady aromas of tropical fruits backed by a lush mouthfeel. The same grape grown in cooler New Zealand, on the other hand, translates to versions that are zippy and mouth-puckeringly tart (and refreshing, I might add), teeming with citrus fruit aromas such as lime and grapefruit. Same grape, completely different personality.

Winemaking Technique

The third factor in determining a wine's style is winemaking technique, something which is most often apparent to tasters in terms of the degree to which oak has been used during the winemaking process. Wines that receive no oak contact at all usually spend all their time in stainless-steel or concrete vats, ultimately going straight into the bottle without ever seeing a hint of wood. Stainless-steel and concrete containers are neutral, meaning that they don't impart any sort of aroma or flavor to the wine. This allows the wines raised in them to retain freshness and the pure fruit character of the grape variety—something that's particularly desirable in many light white wines. Oaked wines, on the other hand, see anywhere from the faintest kiss of oak from used or "neutral" barrels to the full-throttle smack of brand-new high-toast barrels. Because oak imparts aromas and flavors of toast, caramel, and vanilla, it's easy to see how it can radically change the style of a wine.

A great example of this key personality shift can be seen in the marked difference between the faddish new un-oaked Chardonnays—which are rather like zippy Sauvignon Blancs in their crispness—and the full-throttle, high-octane oaked versions from spots like South Australia. And, of course, there are countless degrees of variation in between—as is the case with all wines. The key thing to remember about oak is that it should be used judiciously whenever applied, so that it serves to enhance rather than dominate a wine's delicate aromas and flavors.

The Great Oak Debate

Because wine is a reductive substance, too much contact with oxygen will turn the stuff into vinegar. But small amounts of air slowly released into the wine over long periods of time are actually beneficial, as they encourage the development of the complex aromas and flavors we love so much in mature wines. By this token, the reason oak is used so often in aging red wines is that it's a porous substance that allows tiny amounts of air to seep in over time; this helps the wine continue to evolve as it sits in the barrels.

This is why a very smart guy I know in the wine biz once referred to oak as "a breathing box, not a flavoring box." Which brings up the reason why oak is controversial: It's often used for the wrong reason—for flavoring a wine. This practice was never more clearly abused than when in the nineties mass producers took to flavoring their bland wines with bags of freshly hacked oak chips. Clearly, they were abusing oak to flavor their subpar juice. Which is really too bad, because good quality oak used judiciously in aging a wine can, in addition to giving it much needed air, impart *subtle* aromas and flavors that enhance its overall personality. It's when this subtlety is re-placed with knock-you-over-the-head, fruit-masking oak-iness that things have gone too far.

The Lowdown on Oak

- Unoaked whites and reds are generally the best wines for food.
- Oak should never be used to cover up, or "mask," fruit flavors in wine.
- Porous oak barrels help wines—especially reds—improve over time.
- Good quality oak used *with a light hand* contributes lovely flavors of toast, caramel, and vanilla to wines.
- Wines that work well with oak include Chardonnay, Cabernet Sauvignon, Merlot, and Pinot Noir.

In Defense of Corks

This breathing thing is precisely the reason we use cork—also a porous substance—for wines destined to spend many years in the bottle (top Bordeaux and Napa Cabs come to mind). The same evolution created by a wine's contact with tiny amounts of air while in the barrel continues to occur once a wine is bottled: Over time, small amounts of oxygen seep through the cork and improve the wine. This is why, for wines that are going to spend a good amount of time in a cellar developing layered complexity and delicious nuance, naturally porous cork is hands down the best way to close them up.

Away with TCA! In Support of Screw Caps

For wines that *don't* need to spend years in the bottle, however, screw caps and other alternative closures are much preferred. Why? They remove the possibility of cork taint.

A "corked" wine is one that's been affected by trichloran-isole (TCA), an icky compound found in moldy cork that causes a wine to smell like cardboard and lose its lively fruit flavors. Some experts estimate, in fact, that as much as 7 percent of all wines is affected by TCA. Since the vast majority of wine purchased in America is consumed on the same day it's purchased—as opposed to being squirreled away in a cellar for years to come—the risk of cork taint just isn't worth it.

Table Wines

Now, don't be misled by the simple-sounding name of this category. "Table wine" most definitely does not equal "house wine," the generic stuff bistros often serve in anonymous carafes at rock-bottom prices. The term "table wine," instead, is just a catchall phrase folks apply to wine that's meant to be drunk *at the table*—with food, in other words. Because sweet wines are much more challenging to pair with food—in fact they merit their own category on the subject in Chapter 6—they're not as readily associated with drinking with food as are dry wines, for good reason.

Table wines, on the other hand, are just what you want to reach for when tucking into a meal. So let's review the types of table wines out there and how they come into the world.

The White Stuff

White wine is what you get when you ferment the juice of so-called white grapes. I say "so-called" white grapes because they actually range in color from pale green to gold to rosy pink. No matter: The reason white wine is dubbed "white" is because the juice is pressed immediately out of the skins of the grapes after picking, and therefore does not absorb much color from the skins, as reds and, to a lesser extent, rosé wines do. The juice does, however, invariably take on just a hint of the color of the skins, which is why we have white wines that vary in color from nearly translucent on up to brilliantly deep gold. White table wines vary in style from crisp and citrusy to rich and creamy, and everything in between.

Some Helpful Definitions

Skin contact: When the juice from grapes remains in contact with its skins after pressing; applies to rosé and red wines.

Free-run juice: The first juice to leave the skins of grapes before they are firmly pressed; the best part!

Thinking Pink

Okay, I admit it: I love the color pink. From a die-hard ex-tomboy, it takes a lot for me to admit that. But it's absolutely true, and it's why there's no other wine that makes me as happy as rosé. Call it Barbie wine if you want: Some of it absolutely rocks. How's it made? You'll probably recall from my explanation for the whites that pink wines experience at least *some* contact with the skins of dark grapes during the winemaking process. Also called rosé or blush wines, pink wines are made when so-called red grapes (which, like whites, can vary significantly in hue, in this case from pink to nearly black) are pressed and the juice is allowed to remain in contact with the dark-colored skins for as little as a couple of hours or as long as a couple of days.

> ### A.k.a. Pink Wine
>
> *Rosado* (Spain)
> Rosé (France)
> *Rosato* (Italy)
> Weissherbst (Germany)
> Blush (United States)

Called the *saignée* method in French—which literally means "bled"—this process is what's most often used for good quality pink wine, although the effect can also be achieved by mixing your garden variety white and red wines together. The latter is the budget version (think Bartles & Jaymes), and drinking pink wine made this way is sort of like watching an action movie with really bad special effects; in other words, avoid them! (An exception to this is pink Champagne, but we'll cover that in Chapter 5, "Bubbly Basics and Sweet Treats.")

On the other hand, when made well (i.e., bled), the best pinks are completely dry and offer a combination of floral aromatics, strawberry and watermelon flavors, and a pleasant undercurrent of citrus squirt for food friendliness. They are the ultimate wines of summer. Plus, nothing looks prettier on the table!

Seeing Red

Down with the myth that white wine is for women, red for men! I actually have quite a few girlfriends who've told me over the years that they prefer a smooth red like a Pinot or a French Syrah to a white wine any day. To each her own, I say. Red wines are made when the juice from red grapes spends a good amount of time in contact with the grapes' deeply hued skins, which in turn impart aromas and flavors of red and black fruits, as well as something called tannin. Tannin comes from the skins, stems, and seeds of grapes, and it's what's responsible for that chalky sensation you get on your teeth and gums when you're drinking a really inky, full-throttle red.

The presence of a high level of tannin is why folks will often say of a wine that it's got "chewy tannins." I think the figure of speech is actually quite appropriate, and it brings up a good point about why red wines partner so well with steaks: The chewy texture of tannin is echoed in the tough sinews found in steak. Tannin is also what makes reds capable of aging: It's wine's own natural preservative. A wine that's way too chewy and tannic to be enjoyed when first released, for example, will soften over time (thanks to slow oxygenation, courtesy of the cork) when cellared properly, and come out on the other end a much softer, smoother, and more complex wine.

Of course, there are also reds with low amounts of tannin that are meant to be drunk right away, and there are reds meant for medium-term consumption, too. We'll go into more detail on all this good stuff in Chapter 4.

Weird Wine Stuff Explained

Texture: The feeling of a wine in your mouth. It can range from crisp to creamy to chewy, and is a key factor in wine and food pairing.

Mouthfeel: A synonym for *texture.*

Tannin: The substance in red wine that makes it capable of aging for years in a cellar. Also a key factor in wine and food pairing!

The Others: Sweets and Bubblies

Whew! Are you still with me? Good, because we're making great progress.

It's time to talk about some of my all-time favorite things in the wine world—sweets and bubblies. Or sparklers and stickies, if you prefer those handles. Whatever you call them, sparkling and sweet wines are the unsung divas of the wine world, absolutely gorgeous things that are all too often avoided and criminally underappreciated. Which is a pity, because every time I pour a really kick-ass version of one of them for folks I get the most amazing responses, usually in the form of a widening of the eyes, a smacking of the lips, and a proffering of an empty glass in my direction for another sip of the fabulous stuff.

Bubbly Time

Sparkling wines come in an array of colors, from white to pink to red, and they can also be made by several different methods. The key thing to remember about sparkling wines is that sparkling wines are among the most versatile for pairing with food—the dry versions are, at any rate— and they're hands down the best wines for *starting* things, whether that be a party, a wedding, a luncheon, or just a relaxing evening at home on the couch. Their effervescence, achieved by several methods of bubble creation that we'll go into in more detail in Chapter 5, makes them sing on your palate, while their generally high acidity makes your mouth water for food. This is the definition of a stellar aperitif—or starter beverage—and there's no better aperitif than a great sparkler.

Sweet Stuff

There's a frustrating rumor going around that sweet wines are cheap. This sort of thinking bums me out, because it's completely false. What's worse, it causes good people who might really enjoy them to avoid sweet wines at all costs, which in turn means they miss out on some killer wine and food pairings!

Made by a variety of methods, sweet wines all have this in common: They contain residual sugar in the finished product, which is what makes them sweet. I'll explain the various methods of producing sweet wines in Chapter 5, but for now I'd just like to note that sweet wines absolutely have their place in this world, and when the food pairing's right, they're simply fantastic. I know I said earlier that table wines are the best to serve with food, and I stick by that. However, sweet wines, although less flexible with a broad array of foods, will make your eyes light up when paired properly and on the right occasion; dessert comes readily to mind. But they're also great alone after dinner: The right sweetie can add a fantastic finale to a romantic evening by the fire. I'll leave the rest to you and your special someone.

Quality

As with anything, quality when it comes to wine varies dramatically. The best quality wines, no matter what their style, are those with outstanding balance, meaning that their aromas and flavors and their structural building blocks—including sweetness, acidity, tannin, and alcohol—are integrated harmoniously. No one thing should dominate the whole, in other words. Besides balance, then, the best quality wines also possess unique personalities that make them stand out from their peers. These are the "complete package" wines, and we'll get to know some of the best examples a little later on.

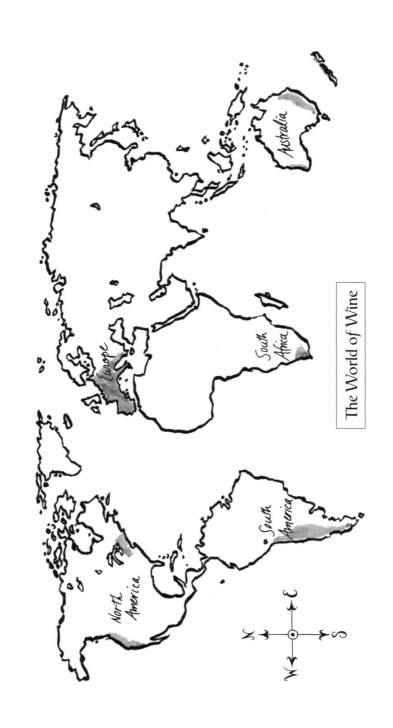

The World of Wine

Hip to Know

Quality does not necessarily correlate directly with price when it comes to wine. In other words, a hefty price tag is never a promise that what's in the bottle will be, in fact, the complete package. I've had just as many superb fifteen-dollar as fifty-dollar wines—you just have to know where to look and whom to trust. More on this later!

Personal Preference

This is not the same as quality: It's far more important! In fact, your personal preference when it comes to wine is the most critical factor in the whole tasting experience. Although I truly believe that the highest quality wines out there—the complete-package wines—are generally appealing on some level to just about every taster, they don't often clock in as folks' favorites. Instead, I find that people tend to gravitate toward certain wines that, for whatever reason, resonate with them personally. As with fashion, film, and art, wine tasting is a subjective thing. This is why my Picasso may in fact be a nine-dollar rosé from a little-known village in Provence, while yours may be a seductive fifty-dollar Brunello di Montalcino from Tuscany. Different quality levels perhaps, but both masterpieces.

It's important to distinguish between quality and personal taste when it comes to wine, because doing so will make you a more sophisticated taster. You ought to be aware of the caliber of the wine in your glass, but by the same token you ought to know and trust your own palate. In other words, be sophisticated, but also be true to yourself. By the end of this book, I hope you'll feel ready to be both.

The Old World/New World Debate

Over the years much has been made about whether a wine hails from the so-called Old World (read: Europe) or the New World (pretty much everywhere else wine is made). I like to think of this distinction in terms of colonialism. Essentially, anyplace that was colonized during the last four or so centuries is a New World region (for example, the United States, Australia, South Africa, and South America). Any spot from which folks set out to colonize other places is considered an Old World region (such as France, Portugal, Spain, and Germany).

Traditionally, Old World wines have been held to possess higher levels of acidity—which makes wine work with food—and more pronounced aromas and flavors of earth and minerals than those from the New World. And it's also been held for a long time that Old World wines—especially reds—are better suited for long-term aging than their New World counterparts. What this really boils down to is climate and vineyard site suitability.

The Role of Climate

The average temperature in many European countries is cooler than that in many New World spots. Consider, for a moment, the climatic difference between brisk Germany and relatively balmy California—two of the world's most famous winegrowing regions. And since it's true that warmer regions generally produce more full-bodied, lower-acid wines, there is some credence to this distinction. However, as New World winemakers discover cooler subregions within their warmer climates, they're increasingly able to make wines that mimic the lower alcohol and higher acidity of Old World wines.

Another key factor is global warming, which—especially in the last ten or twelve years—has led to a gradual upswing of temperatures in many of Europe's coolest winegrowing regions. The wines produced there, as a result, are increasingly beginning to resemble those made in warmer parts of the world.

Vineyard Site Suitability

At the same time, New World regions such as Australia, Argentina, and the United States have made impressive strides in locating plots of land ideally suited to growing specific wine grapes. This is something that can be achieved only by a process of elimination—which takes time. And while New World winemakers are just beginning to get a leg up on the process, their Old World counterparts have had the good fortune of fine-tuning their vine/land suitability over thousands of years.

A Convergence of Styles

The discovery of better vineyard sites in the New World and warming climates in the Old mean that it's becoming less and less important to pay attention to the Old World/ New World distinction. At the end of the day, ideal vineyard sites, whether in Europe or abroad, tend to be mineral-rich and to produce layered, complex wines that pair beautifully with food and, well, taste fantastic. They're also capable of producing wines that will age beautifully in the bottle, a quality that often has as much to do with the grape variety in question and the skill of the winemaker as it does with the vineyard site.

The bottom line: The stylistic line between Old World and New World regions has begun to blur. Still, I'll refer to it in this book because it's widely used in the wine world as a general distinction. My advice: Take it with a grain of salt.

Naming: Place Versus Grape

There's a fundamental divide in the wine world when it comes to naming the good stuff, and fortunately for those of us who'd like to get a handle on the subject, it falls neatly along the Old World/New World divide.

Old World regions like France and Italy (see pages 91 and 105) have traditionally named their wines after the places where they're grown. Consider, for example, Champagne and Bordeaux, two of the most famous wine regions in France, which also lend their names to the wines made there. New World regions like the United States and Australia, on the other hand, have developed a system of varietal labeling that takes its cues from the major grape varieties of the world. So, rather than reaching for a bottle of Bordeaux, we may reach instead for a bottle of Cabernet Sauvignon from Napa. Cab's the same grape that goes into many Bordeaux reds, but we just think of it in a different way—by the name of the grape itself.

Neither naming system is right or wrong; they're just different. Unfortunately, this difference can result in a lot of confusion for shoppers who tend to be more familiar with one naming system over the other. Americans, for obvious reasons, tend to recognize wines based on grape variety, and as a result we find ourselves scratching our heads in the wine shop as we attempt to puzzle out what's in a Sancerre (Sauvignon Blanc) or a Chianti (Sangiovese). Lucky for you I've broken all of this out in Chapters 3 and 4, so that you'll know next time that a Burgundy is really just a Pinot Noir with a little je ne sais quoi thrown in for good measure.

All About Place

Appellation: A geographic location where wine is made; usually regulated by local laws and listed on most bottles of wine. In the United States, we call these AVAs—American Viticultural Areas.

Lieu-dit: Literally, "named place" in French. Refers to a specific subregion within an appellation that is not recognized by law.

Vintages Debunked

Technically speaking, the word "vintage" refers to the year in which the grapes making up a particular bottle of wine were harvested. It can also refer to a special bottling of wine—most often Champagne—made entirely from grapes from a single year's harvest (versus non-vintage Champagne, a blend of several years' worth of grapes). No matter where it's from, when a wine is made up entirely of grapes from a single year's harvest, we call it a "vintage wine."

What's the Big Deal?

If you're anything like me, hearing someone go on and on about what a "great year" 2005 was in Bordeaux is enough to make your eyes roll back in your head. However, there are some good reasons to at least take note of a wine's vintage, chief among them being to avoid getting something unpalatable and unpleasant!

Why do people care about vintages in the first place? Certain wine-growing regions—especially cooler areas like Germany—can experience dramatic weather variation from year to year. These fluctuations affect the quality of wine produced there, and as a result it can really help to have at least a basic grasp of recent "good" vintages from these regions, so you can avoid unwittingly picking up an unsatisfying bottle from an off year. To assist you with this I've included in the Appendix a list of recommended recent vintages so that you can know what to seek out—and what to avoid!

The Three-Year Rule

And here's an easy-to-remember rule of thumb for white wines: Most whites—except a very few that actually improve with time—are meant to be drunk within three years of their release. In fact, some of the most crisp and lively whites, like New Zealand Sauvignon Blanc, are at their best almost immediately after release. This is why I avoid most white wines on restaurant lists that are more than three years old. Wondering what the exceptions are? You'll often know by the price—they're the expensive ones!

Cellar-Worthy Wines

Another consideration when it comes to vintages is the age-worthiness of a wine. For wines that will improve for years in a cellar (e.g., vintage port, some California Cabs, Bordeaux from France), vintage is one of the main criteria collectors use in determining which wines will stand the test of time. Only those from the best years, such as, yes, 2005 in Bordeaux, have the ripeness of tannin and the "complete package" structure to last. Wines that don't have these goodies—which are chiefly determined by vintage year—will break down in the cellar and lose their charm long before you have a chance to pop the cork.

Personally, I don't have a wine cellar of my own, so the "wine for cellaring" issue isn't as relevant for me. However, it's nice to know why it's important, even if it's not of the utmost relevance to you at the moment. And after all, you never know when you'll be given the opportunity to choose a bottle of wine in some gazillionaire's fancy cellar during a party (it has been known to happen). Won't it be nice if you can reach right for the '61 Pétrus, knowing it's one of the all-time winners of the world's wine scene over the past, oh, one hundred years? Whether or not your host lets you open it is another question entirely.

The Great Strawberry Debate

I'll never forget the time my good friend Jen asked me if the winemaker had really added strawberries to the wine we were drinking. We were enjoying a Pinot Noir from France's famed Burgundy, and I'd just described it as smelling of "dried cherries, strawberries, and baking spice."

I probably laughed for a solid minute at her question.

At the time Jen was working for one of the top strategy consulting firms in the country. Though she's clearly a bright gal, her question—which seemed silly to me back then (doesn't everyone know the only thing that goes into wine is grapes?!)—brings up a great point about wine: It seems to defy logic.

In all likelihood Jen's inspiration for the strawberry question is rooted firmly in our notions of cooking. It makes sense: When cooking you mix together various ingredients before coming up with a finished product that encompasses essences of all of them. Wine, on the other hand, manages to smell and taste of many goodies (including strawberries), but is in fact made from just a single thing: grapes. Looking back on Jen's question, I feel a little guilty for laughing at her. Thankfully, she's forgiven me and we're still friends—probably because I continue to share lots of ridiculously good wines with her, minus the laughter.

Chapter 2

Taste Like a Pro

All About Volatility

In this chapter I'll explain how wine manages to wear so many aromatic and flavor hats, and I'll highlight the major aromas and flavors you can expect to find in most wines. I'll also decode the awkward-seeming activity that is wine tasting (clue: The gurgling is actually a good thing!). Finally, I'll wrap with some sample tasting notes so that, should you choose, you can begin keeping a record of your own tasting adventures. You'll remember what you've tasted, but never make a strawberry blunder of your own.

Wine is one of the most volatile substances we consume. And no, that doesn't mean it's prone to late-night drunken romps, nor does it have a rap sheet longer than your last cell phone bill. Instead, when we talk about volatility in wine we're just talking about its remarkable ability to transmit aromas. Generally speaking, the more volatile a food or drink, the more aromas it gives off. Foods that have been heated up, for example, are made more volatile by the heat and transmit far more smells than they do when cool. Wine, however, does not need to be heated up to send off a fabulously vast array of scents. This is a major reason why we love the stuff so much!

Tasting Wine: What Are You Looking For?

Learning to taste wine like a pro will help you assess the quality of what's in your glass and add to your enjoyment of the stuff. As an activity, tasting wine is definitely different from just drinking it. *Tasting* wine is different chiefly in that you're actively considering the components of a wine rather than just knocking it back. Not that there's anything wrong with drinking wine for pleasure! Instead, I just want to highlight the fact that tasting wine based on the following technique can, although it requires a bit more concentration, greatly increase your enjoyment and understanding of it. Actively tasting takes a little longer, to be sure, but it's absolutely worth it.

There are three things we consider when tasting a wine: the way it looks, the way it smells, and the way it tastes. Some people shorthand this to "sight, smell, and taste," which is fine by me, although I prefer the slightly more snobby-sounding but in reality more accurate monikers "appearance, nose, and palate."

Histamines: How to Deal

As I am a huge wine fan, it makes me sad to hear about friends and acquaintances who report getting sick after drinking wine. Histamines are the substances found in red wines that are believed to be responsible for giving some unlucky tasters headaches and other icky symptoms after drinking. Fortunately, taking an over-the-counter antihistamine a few hours before you know you'll be tasting has proven successful in helping some folks overcome the problem.

Appearance: The Way It Looks

Wine comes in many shades besides your everyday red and white. In addition to these two common descriptors, wine can be nearly translucent, straw-colored, green yellow, golden, amber, garnet, ruby, purple, inky black, and, you guessed it, everything in between. The color of a wine contains clues about its quality and its age. Red wines tend to become lighter in color as they age, while white wines become darker over time. Eventually, as I've observed in some truly old examples of both red and white wines, they begin to look very much the same—a sort of deep amber color. Young wines, like most that you and I encounter in our everyday drinking, tend to retain most of their original color.

Women Make Better Tasters

A study conducted by the Clinical Smell and Taste Research Center of the University of Pennsylvania proved as much when women outperformed men on taste tests in every age group examined. In another study, Linda Bartoshuk, professor at the Yale University School of Medicine, showed that all tasters can be divided into three tiers of tasting ability: nontasters, regular tasters, and supertasters. Supertasters are defined as the lucky folks who possess up to one hundred times as many taste buds as their less well budded peers. Guess who makes up the lion's share of the supertaster contingent? You got it: chicks. The upside, for the gents, is that practice has proven to make up for a good deal of the natural advantage the ladies have.

In terms of quality, the appearance of the wine in your glass should be clear, not cloudy or speckled with sediment. Cloudy or hazy wines are usually flawed wines, although you're highly unlikely to happen upon any of these nowadays, since modern winemaking technology ensures that most of our wines appear crystal clear to the eye. Sediment, on the other hand, is not necessarily a bad thing in wine, although this harmless substance is ideally filtered out via a funnel or by decanting before you consume it. In terms of appearance, sediment usually shows up as grainy or chunky particles floating in the bottle or your glass. Should you see the occasional particle, though, don't sweat it! Finally, take a quick mental note of the wine's color; we'll learn more about the various grapes and their "signature" colors in the next chapter.

Taking It All In

In order to best assess a wine's color, tilt your glass slightly and hold it against a white background (your garden variety white napkin will do the trick). It's best to look at wine against a white surface, because colored backgrounds distort its appearance. What are you looking for? Look for differences between the color in the middle of the glass (the core) and that at the edge (the rim). Generally speaking, older and lighter bodied wines tend to have greater variation between the wine in the middle of your glass and that at the edge.

Also worth noting are the wine's "legs." Swirl the wine in your glass and watch how it runs down the sides. If it moves slowly back down your glass in heavy streams (legs), it's likely that the wine has a high alcohol content, the chief thing responsible for forming legs, or "tears," as they're also often called. Alcohol serves to make wines fatter or bigger in body, and this is what you're observing when looking at the legs. Legs can also indicate an elevated sugar content. Wines such as port that have both high alcohol *and* high sugar content tend to have the most noticeable legs, as you might imagine. As far as the myth that legs are an indicator of quality—that's an old wives' tale.

Aroma: The Way It Smells

We can infer more about a wine from the way it smells than we can from anything else we evaluate while tasting. A wine's aromas give us clues as to whether it's young or has some age on it, whether it's healthy or flawed, which grape variety or varieties it includes, and which winemaking techniques were used in crafting it. Smelling a wine is my favorite part of the whole exercise, due to wine's prolifically smelly nature: Your average glass of wine is teeming with tons of these delicious aromas just begging for you to sort them out.

To do so, swirl the wine a bit in the glass—this will stir up its aromas and allow you to get a good whiff. If you're opposed to swirling on the grounds that it looks uppity and pretentious, you're destined to miss out on the lion's share of pleasure a glass of wine affords! So swirl away, my friend. Then, stick your nose into the glass (again, it looks a little awkward, but it's so worth it) and inhale deeply. What do you smell? Wine tasting is totally subjective, so there's no wrong answer.

Love at First Scent

Just as some people report powerful reactions to their first sighting of a potential mate, our first whiff of a glass of wine tells us much more about its character than any subsequent sniffs. This is because the scent receptors in our noses act like matches, which glow most brightly just after they're struck. Similarly, once our smelling receptors are stimulated, they snuff out briefly while synthesizing the first whiff. Any subsequent smells have dramatically less impact in helping us identify what we're smelling. So with wine it truly *is* love (or whatever you feel about the stuff) at first scent.

The Nose: Pinch Hitter for the 'Buds

Besides being prolifically smelly (in a good way), wine can smell like many different things besides just grapes. We can thank its high level of volatility for this chameleonic capacity to smell like berry fruits one moment and leather and spice the next. And while we humans can smell as many as ten thousand different aromas, we can actually taste only five things: sweetness, saltiness, sourness, bitterness, and something called *umami,* which means "savory" in Japanese. Shocking, isn't it, this obscenely short list of things we can taste?! I know it seems terrifically odd, so allow me to clarify.

Rather than *tasting* things we put in our mouths, we're actually *smelling* them. Our chief organ for smelling things—called the olfactory bulb (I know, *so* not sexy sounding)—is situated in the upper reaches of the nasal passage, a channel that connects, conveniently, to the back of the throat. When we're tasting something, what we're really doing is vaporizing it, courtesy of the oxygen in our mouths, and sending its aromas up our interior nasal passage to the olfactory bulb, which sorts it out into what we commonly know as "flavors." This is why you'll see professional tasters gurgling the wine in their mouths before swallowing: They're just stimulating the mixing of oxygen and the good stuff! And they're better for it, although I definitely don't recommend gurgling at a cocktail party any time soon.

Now that we know about the nose's primary role in tasting wine, I want to make sure you don't discount the mouth as entirely deficient when it comes to tasting. Our mouths, it turns out, play the critical role of assessing a wine's structure, something that's vital to determining the style and quality of a wine. The key building blocks of structure—a wine's acid, alcohol, and tannin levels, as well as any residual sugar content it may possess—are vital players in creating a clear picture of a wine's personality. We'll go over just how these things are ID'd and sorted out a little later on, but for now just remember that the mouth's got this part covered.

Aromatherapy: The Power of Scent

Our sense of smell is closely related to our capacity for memory, with its neurological receptor located right smack next to that of memory in our brains. This is probably why wine tasting is so often dubbed an "emotional" pursuit: The countless aromas found in wine trigger emotional responses based on past associations we have with various scents. This is why a floral, fresh-smelling German Riesling may remind you of a meadow picnic you particularly enjoyed in the past or a bouquet of flowers you gave your sweetie on V Day.

Common Aromas

Scents of vanilla and toast can often be attributed to oak used in the wine's maturation process, while fruit flavors such as berries and tropical fruits can be attributed to the grape variety (e.g., Pinot Noir and Chardonnay, respectively). You might also smell earthiness, herbs, and aromas of coffee, smoke, leather, and flowers. The list is endless. Like I said before, there's no wrong answer, and if you're convinced you smell bubble gum or pine cones or licorice in a wine, then good for you. I would probably congratulate you if you were in one of my classes!

Flaws, on the other hand, will make a wine smell musty, vinegary, acrylic, and all sorts of other icky things. Generally speaking, flaws are tricky for folks other than pros to identify, but I find that most novice tasters can at least tell that a wine tastes "off" or "wrong." If this is the case for a wine you're tasting, I recommend pouring it out and starting afresh. Life's too short to drink bad wine.

Common Wine Flaws

Brettanomyces ("Brett")—a spoilage yeast found on some grapes and in wine.
Smells like: barnyard, sweaty saddle, wet dog, Band-Aid

2,4,6-trichloranisole ("TCA")—a foul-smelling compound caused by chlorine contamination of corks; affected wines are called "corked."
Smells like: wet cardboard, musty attic

Volatile acidity ("VA")—the overproduction of acetic acid and ethyl acetate in wine.

Smells like: nail polish remover, vinegar, paint thinner

Mercaptans—caused by the improper handling of sulfur-based products during winemaking.
Smells like: rotten eggs

Palate: The Way It Tastes

Now, the good part. Take a sip of the wine and swish it around in your mouth, pausing for a moment before swallowing. This will allow the wine to coat all the surfaces of your mouth. Because different parts of our mouths perceive different structural and flavor elements, it makes sense that you've got to give the wine a good swishing to fully experience all of these things. Again, you've probably seen the gurglers doing this swishing thing, too; it is, like the gurgling, a good thing when it comes to fully appreciating a wine, although it's better done in the privacy of your own home than at your next office party!

The first thing you want to consider when tasting a wine is its structure, which is why tasting has a lot more to do with texture—with feeling—than it does with flavors. We perceive sweetness on the tip of our tongue, acidity on the sides, and tannin most often on our teeth and gums. Tannin is the same drying substance found in tea; sucking on a tea bag would give you roughly the same sensation as quaffing a high-tannin wine. (I know, thoroughly unpleasant sounding!) Alcohol shows up in a wine in the form of body (wines with higher alcohol contents taste fatter or more creamy than lower alcohol versions) as well as by the sensation of heat.

Flavor Fun

Once you've considered the structural components of a wine it's time to take a moment to ponder its flavors. Although we know that flavors are synthesized and sorted out in the olfactory bulb, we still consider them part of the tasting experience. Some things to look for are fruit flavors—reds tend to taste like red berry fruits including strawberries and raspberries, while whites often taste like citrus fruits such as lemons and tropical fruits like bananas. Besides fruit, you might also taste toast, cocoa, pepper, or herbs, depending on what's in your glass. Finally, consider the wine's finish. Wines that you can taste for some time after you swallow (up to several minutes for the best wines) are considered to have good length. The "longest" wines, as we like to say, are usually of the best quality.

Sample Tasting Note: A White

2005 L'École N° 41 Sémillon, Washington State, United States

Appearance: Golden straw with translucent rim.

Nose: This pretty wine jumps out of the glass with luscious aromas of melon, tropical fruits, flowers, orange essence, and caramel.

Palate: If possible, the palate is even more lush, with rich peach, apricot, pear, and baking spice flavors. The finish is long. Perfect for the "big" white wine fans! Practically a meal in and of itself.

Sample Tasting Note: A Rosé

2004 Château Val Joanis, Côtes du Lubéron, France

Appearance: Lovely peach core with lighter rim.

Nose: Fresh aromas of nectarines, apricots, meadow grass, and chamomile make this pretty-hued wine smell like summer itself; there's also a nutty essence.

Palate: Flavors echo the nose and include notes of baked apricot and more grassy freshness, this time underpinned by hints of herbs and lemon squirt. The finish is of moderate length. A simple, pleasant summer quaffer.

Sample Tasting Note: A Red

2004 Paul Hobbs El Felino Malbec, Mendoza, Argentina

Appearance: Deep ruby–colored core with brick rim.

Nose: Pretty aromas of blackberry, black cherry, and blueberry leave little wonder why Malbec is often referred to as a "black" grape. Also dried roses, pipe tobacco, granite, leather, licorice, toast, and plum notes.

Palate: Lip-smackingly ripe fruit flavors dominate the palate. Raspberry, blackberry, plum, and cherry lead the charge, followed by more subtle notes of toasty oak, vanilla, tobacco, smoke, and pepper. The long finish is mouth-coatingly broad, and wraps up with smoke.

Final Thoughts: Balance and Quality

As I mentioned before, the best wines are what's called "balanced," meaning that their structural building blocks, including sweetness, acidity, tannin, and alcohol levels, are all in sync, with no one thing overwhelming the others. Besides this, their flavor profiles are appealing and multi-dimensional. Or, more simply put, the best wines taste harmonious, well knit, and pleasant. Again, a wine's quality isn't nearly as important as your personal take on it, but as mentioned earlier, it's wonderful to be able to accurately evaluate the two—quality and personal preference—and then make a well-guided decision on what you like best, armed with all the information of a savvy taster.

Saints and Sinners

I once hosted a terrifically successful tasting of light white wines and big, full-bodied reds called Saints and Sinners. I played up contrasts between the white and red wines, referring to the whites as ethereal and saintly and the reds as dark and, well, sinful. Slotting the wines into these playful contexts made them somehow more accessible to guests, who packed the San Francisco venue and stayed late into the night swirling, sampling, and merrymaking.

What I enjoyed most about the Saints and Sinners tasting was the opportunity it gave me to show off white wines on an equal—and opposite—footing with reds. All too often whites are overshadowed by their more showy counterparts, red wines, which by no fault of their own seem to get the lion's share of the wine world's limelight. Thus eclipsed, white wines are often dismissed as afterthoughts, as things you knock back before getting to the *real* wines— big, powerful reds.

In reality, the world of whites includes some of the most complex and fascinating wines out there, and in this chapter I'll tell you all about these gems as well as a group of lesser-known but still stellar white varieties. Each is described in terms of its common aromas and flavors, the key regions where it's grown, and whether it appears mostly as a varietal wine (solo artist) or as part of a blend (backup). And don't believe the reds-are-better hype: Lots of whites are *sinfully* good.

Chapter 3

The White Stuff

There are a handful of white grapes that turn up again and again on store shelves, restaurant lists, and everywhere else quality wine can be found. These include popular favorites Chardonnay and Sauvignon Blanc as well as lesser-known gems such as Riesling, Viognier, and Chenin Blanc. Because I'd never dream of discriminating, this chapter profiles the most popular whites as well as those that often show up in supporting roles or are just breaking into the global wine scene in a big way.

The Major Players

Riesling: The Black Sheep
Status: Solo Star
If there were a wine shrine at which I worshipped, it would undoubtedly be at one for the Riesling grape. And although

names like Blue Nun and Liebfraumilch put a serious
dent in its reputation over the last thirty or so years
(hence the "Black Sheep" moniker), this darling of the
sommelier community is currently making a comeback in
a big way.

Here's why: Riesling boasts naturally high acidity—
which is ideal for food pairing—alongside a gorgeous
lightness of body and stunning aromatics. Which means it
doesn't knock you over the head with its crispness like
some other high-acid whites can. Moreover, Riesling
doesn't get in the way of food with high alcohol (it doesn't
have it), overextraction (doesn't go through it), or oakiness
(it never sees new oak). This is why I often refer to it as a
"clean" wine.

And with Riesling springing up on a growing number
of wine lists across the land, more and more consumers are
catching the Riesling bug. The best versions hail from
Germany and France's easterly Alsace, although some excellent Rieslings can also be found in Austria, California,
Washington State, and Australia.

Lowdown on the Sweet Thing

Yes, it's true: Riesling is often sweet. Many of the best versions from Germany, in fact, are sweet to varying degrees
(there are actually six levels of sweetness set down by law
there—that's how serious they are about their sweetness).
This sweetness, especially at the lower end of the sugar
scale, actually serves to mitigate the tart acidity naturally
present in Riesling grapes. In other words, the sweetness
makes many Rieslings more balanced.

And, contrary to popular belief, sweetness is *the* thing to
drink with some of our favorite ethnic foods, like Thai,
because spicy and sweet flavors tend to work terrifically
well together. A good analogy is the role of a cooling yogurt sauce with a terrifically spicy Indian dish. Riesling's
sweetness plays the same mellowing role as the yogurt
sauce. More on this in Chapter 6.

Six Levels of Sweetness in German Wines

Kabinett: The lightest style of the sweet German wines, Kabinett wines are only slightly sweet and tend to be very floral, low in alcohol, and some of the best table wines for food, bar none.

Spätlese: A step up in terms of sweetness from Kabinett, Spätlese wines still have great balance; stylistically, they're sandwiched between table wines and dessert wines.

Auslese: Full-bodied and rich, Auslese wines are made from late-harvested grapes that may even have a kiss of the friendly fungus *Botrytis* ("noble rot"). These are definitely dessert-wine caliber in terms of sweetness, and are rare to boot.

Beerenauslese: Made only in the best years from supersweet, fully shriveled (nobly rotted) grapes, Beerenauslese is a full-blown, honeyed dessert wine that's something worth trying in this lifetime.

Eiswein: Similar to Beerenauslese in terms of sweetness but made from frozen grapes. Very rare and always expensive, these wines marry intense sweetness with racy acidity, making them some of the most expressive dessert wines around.

Trockenbeerenauslese (TBA): Made from fully shriveled, handpicked *Botrytis*-affected grapes, TBA wines are nutty brown in color and so sweet their texture has been compared to cough syrup. Unbelievably complex and obscenely rare.

The Bottom Line

Riesling is refreshing, elegant, and expressive and doesn't need to grab your attention with the likes of one-trick ponies like overwhelming oak and obscenely high alcohol. It comes in dramatically varied versions, including completely dry styles, slightly sweet incarnations, and full-blown dessert wine renderings. All this, and it's dynamite with some of the toughest foods to pair with wine, including sashimi. What else could a budding oenophile want?

When to Drink?

Riesling is almost always raised in either stainless-steel or old neutral wood barrels. White wines made in this way (Sauvignon Blanc from outside California also comes to mind) retain a crisp fruitiness that makes them the most refreshing wines out there. Riesling is generally ready to drink right after it's released, although some of the better bottlings can be absolutely wonderful after as much as ten to twenty years in the cellar.

Aromas and Flavors

Riesling is fabulously aromatic. In fact, it's one of a family of grapes often referred to affectionately as "the aromatic whites." You'll probably recall from the last chapter that I said much of our appreciation of wine comes from smelling it? Well, you don't have to be a Mensa candidate to infer that Riesling—as possibly the *most* aromatic white grape out there—packs tons of layered floral, fruit, and mineral scents for us to enjoy. In fact, I find that drinking one calls to mind walking near a fresh mountain stream (minerality in wine is often described as smelling of wet stones) bordered by flowers.

Common Aromas

Citrus fruits: candied lemon and lime
Pome fruits: apple, pear
Stone fruits: apricot, peach
Tropical fruits: banana, pineapple
Also: wet stones, slate, melon, gasoline (seriously)

Common Flavors

Citrus fruits: candied lemon and lime
Pome fruits: apple, pear
Stone fruits: apricot, peach
Tropical fruits: banana, pineapple
Also: mineral, melon, honey

Home Sweet Home

Germany: Moselle, Nahe, Pfalz, Rheingau
Austria
France: Alsace
Australia
United States: Washington, California, New York

Blends: Watch for It In

Nada: Riesling almost always performs alone.

Sauvignon Blanc: The Comeback Kid
Status: Solo Star and Backup
Sauvignon Blanc has been turning heads both as a solo star and in blends for hundreds of years, but what's most remarkable about this versatile varietal is its recent makeover as the trendiest wine of the new millennium. Aficionados know it as the solo star of Sancerre and Pouilly-Fumé, the classic white wines made in France's castle-studded Loire Valley that have long graced the wine lists of the toniest restaurants.

But today's drinkers more readily associate it with the zippy incarnations coming out of hip New Zealand, a new wine region by historical standards—which means it's been producing wine for decades rather than millennia. How's it different? New Zealand Sauvignon Blanc is varietally labeled, which makes it more approachable on supermarket shelves than Sancerre (which takes its name from a place versus a grape), and its style is a bit more brisk than Sancerre's creamier rendering. But otherwise, these crisp and light versions are quite similar.

Things get different when we talk about Sauvignon Blanc from California. We can thank California wine pioneer Robert Mondavi for introducing the oaked style of Sauvignon Blanc we see so often from the Golden State under the moniker "Fumé Blanc." "Fumé" means "smoked" in French, a term that's a little misleading as there isn't much of a smoky essence to these wines. Instead, they're full-bodied whites more reminiscent of lush Chardonnay than of French or New Zealand Sauvignons. This is due to a combination of higher alcohol content (courtesy of California's warmer climate) and a more intensive winemaking style.

Playing Dress-up:
Lees Stirring and Use of Oak

While I'll readily admit that I prefer crisp, unoaked versions of Sauvignon Blanc to the gussied-up oaked versions from California, that's not to say that there aren't some made in the latter style that are quite tasty. The thing that saves these wines from being unpalatably fat is the very nature of the Sauvignon grape. Its high level of natural acidity gives it a *bright* quality, so even after a producer has doused it with brand-new high-toast barrels and put it through an additional fattening-up process called lees stirring, it usually manages to perk up from underneath all this makeup with a refreshing undercurrent of acid.

Lees Stirring 411

This is a technique used frequently for some of the better oaked white wines, although it can be done to excess. It happens when the wine is in barrels, and involves, essentially, the periodic mixing up of the wine with the dead yeast cells and other sediment (collectively, the "lees") that are the by-products of the winemaking process. As wine sits in a barrel, particles settle out of the liquid portion of the juice. Stirring them up encourages the commingling of the lees and the juice and lends added complexity and a trademark creaminess to the finished wine. But because it's labor intensive, it adds up—as you might guess—to a higher price tag for these wines.

The Bottom Line

Whether fortified with some toasty oak or left in its crisp, lean state, Sauvignon Blanc makes a refreshing white wine that's ideally suited to food. Unlike floral Riesling, however, Sauvignon Blanc tends toward vegetal aromas and flavors and, accordingly, is ideally suited to a whole different array of foods. And, because it's so crisp, it makes a perfect aperitif (before-dinner drink). Zippy wines with a good dose of acidity like Sauvignon Blanc perk up our taste buds and make our mouths water—which is the ideal state to be in just before tucking into a meal. This same crispness is also what makes Sauvignon the perfect partner for shellfish, fried foods (its mouthwatering acidity plays the same role as a squirt of lemon on your fish and chips), and green salads—nearly impossible to partner with wine.

When to Drink?

Sauvignon Blanc is best drunk young, ideally within three years of its release. Unlike Riesling, whose apricot and peach flavors can evolve into really lovely honeyed notes with age, Sauvignon Blanc's vegetal and citrus-fruit-driven flavors tend to grow mute and lose their charm with age. This is why the best Sauvignons are usually the youngest, and it's also why I avoid those I see on restaurant wine lists and retail shelves that are more than three years old.

Aromas and Flavors

Well known for its assertive aromas, Sauvignon Blanc often smells of freshly cut grass, grapefruit, and lime, as well as the critics' favorite Sauvignon smell, cat's pee. Hardly appealing, this infamous descriptor is controversial, but is in fact something that's detectable in some of the more pungent renderings of the grape. Others refer to the same smell as gooseberry; having never sampled a gooseberry but having grown up with many a feline, I stick by the cat's pee. Sound unpleasant? It's really not; it's so muted, in fact, compared with the real thing that it's laughable.

Common Aromas

Citrus fruits: grapefruit, lemon, lime
Greenness: freshly cut grass, honeysuckle, rainforest,
    freshness
Minerality: slate, wet stones

Common Flavors

Citrus fruits: grapefruit, lemon, lime
Greenness: tomato, herbs, bell pepper
Also: mineral, toast (if oaked), melon, passion fruit

Home Sweet Home

France: Loire Valley, Bordeaux
Australia
Chile
South Africa
United States: California
New Zealand

Blends: Watch for It In

White table wines from Bordeaux, where it's blended
    with full-bodied Sémillon
Sweet dessert wines from around the world, blended
    with Sémillon and others
Sauternes (Bordeaux)
Ice wine (Canada)

Chardonnay: The Chameleon
Status: Solo Star and Backup

The basis for Chardonnay's popularity is its impressive ability to conform to just about any setting and any winemaking technique. It's grown successfully pretty much everywhere
wine grapes grow (a rarity), something that's possible because it can adapt to innumerable *terroirs*. All this and it
makes lovely wines in both oaked and unoaked styles.

Malo-*what*?

Malolactic fermentation (sometimes referred to as
"MLF") is a common step during the winemaking
process for most red wines and some whites, especially Chardonnay. During the process, harsh malic
acid—naturally present in new wine—is converted
to the softer, more desirable lactic acid. To give you

some points of flavor reference, malic acid is what's naturally present in tart green apples, whereas lactic acid can be found in milk and yogurt. The process is carried out by the addition of lactic bacteria to the wine, and occurs after the primary, or alcoholic, fermentation. Wines that have undergone MLF can sometimes smell of cream or butter—no surprise given what we now know about lactic acid. And just like any other winemaking process, MLF can be abused by feeble-minded winemakers who use it to cover up undesirable aromas and flavors in their wines. If you can smell cream but not fruit in your wine, that's probably what's been done.

The Backstory

Because Chardonnay harmonizes so well with oak, odious winemakers with few scruples and a desire to make big bucks took to dousing their Chardonnays with oak chips to impart inexpensively the essence of oak. Oak chips, unlike the real thing (high quality oak barrels), taste sawdusty and overpowering, and serve only, in the end, to create cheap-tasting wine. By contrast, good quality oak barrels, when used in concert with juice from healthy Chardonnay vines, can create wines of subtlety and complexity that are prized by collectors and smart people the world over.

The Bottom Line

Chardonnay is a flexible grape whose assets have been abused in the past but is, fortunately, making a comeback. In some instances this is in the form of bright unoaked versions that still show the weight and charm of this medium-bodied white but without the intrusion of oak. At the same time, intelligent winemakers are keen to the fact that many people in fact *do* like oaked Chardonnay, but only when it's been done right. As a result they're using good quality oak barrels and avoiding excessive manipulation in the winery to craft suave oaked versions. These are among the top wines of the world.

The best versions—oaked or unoaked—partner beautifully with rich white fish and shellfish, including lobster and scallops, and stand up remarkably well to pasta and chicken. Watch for crisp versions from France's famous Chablis, rich renderings from France's Burgundy (see Appendix for help with choosing wines from both Chablis and Burgundy), and some outstanding New World incarnations from Australia and California.

A Question of Toastiness: How Much Is Too Much?

Oak comes from many locations, chief among them France and America, although versions from Portugal and Eastern Europe are also popular.

There are three main levels of toastiness when it comes to winemaking: light toast, medium toast, and heavy toast. Depending on how much toasting's been done, your finished wine will have a corresponding degree of oak intensity, which usually shows up in the form of aromas and flavors of vanilla, clove, caramel, spice, and, you guessed it, toast.

The question of how much is too much is really a personal one. Some people prefer a subtle whiff of vanilla on their wine (probably from light-toast barrels), while others like it when they're greeted by a nothing-shy-about-me blast of spice from their glass (I'm guessing high toast here!). My only caveat to the personal preference rule is that it's critical that you can taste the *fruit* from the Chardonnay grape underneath all this other stuff. The wine should also be refreshing and taste good with food—two things that fall by the wayside when too much toasting's been done.

When to Drink?

Drink unoaked Chardonnays as soon as possible, as they're meant to be enjoyed young and fresh. Oaked versions from top producers in the best regions for Chardonnay (for example, California's Sonoma and France's Burgundy) are capable of aging, but only the *very best* of this group will improve beyond five or so years in a cellar. Proceed with caution, as the best are usually the most expensive.

Aromas and Flavors

The Chardonnay grape in its pure (read: unoaked) form smells of apples, pears, lemon squirt, and, if from a warmer climate, tropical fruits, including bananas and pineapples. Its style changes dramatically based on where its grown. Cool climate versions from France's famous Chablis lean toward the apple and lemon side, and warmer climate renderings from California and Australia incorporate richer nuances of the tropical fruit nature. Wherever they're made, oaked versions will incorporate the typical toast, vanilla, and spice notes of oak.

Common Aromas

Pome fruits: apple, pear
Tropical fruits: banana, pineapple
Also: vanilla, butter, cream, baking spices, lemon or
    lime, toast, oak, hazelnut

Common Flavors

Pome fruits: apple, pear
Tropical fruits: banana, pineapple
Also: vanilla, butter, cream, baking spices, citrus fruit,
    toast, hazelnut

Home Sweet Home

France: Chablis, Burgundy's Côte d'Or
Australia
Argentina
United States: California, Oregon, Washington

Blends: Watch for It In

Champagne, baby

Other White Players

Chenin Blanc
Status: Solo Star and Backup

Ah, poor Chenin. At one time prized as one of the finest white wines in the world, it's lately taken a sad turn toward unpopularity, due to the overproduction of cheap sweetened versions in its native France. Which is too bad, because these unworthies overshadow the lovely qualities of the best versions of the grape: Great Chenins incorporate the crisp acidity and approachable charm of this medium-bodied white, and are outstanding with food.

With its unmistakable aromas of flowers, honey, red apples, and lemon squirt, Chenin Blanc is sometimes compared to Chardonnay. It packs a bigger acidic punch than most Chardonnays, however, which is why it's so darned food friendly. Dry versions of Chenin Blanc are capable of improving for as much as twenty or more years after bottling, in fact—a rare feat for a white wine (we can thank the strong dose of acid for this age worthiness)! The best of these age-worthy charmers hail from the appellation of Savennières in France's Loire Valley—also home to Sancerre and Pouilly-Fumé. Nearby Vouvray produces some outstanding versions as well, although none can touch the age worthiness of the best Savennières.

Chenin also comes in some good sweet versions, the

best of which are the fabulous dessert wines from the Loire's Coteaux du Layon and Bonnezeaux. Sparkling Chenin is produced by the boatload in the Loire, and some of it is delicious. For the best stuff, watch for bottlings that say "Crémant de Loire" on the label. In terms of food, dry Chenins work beautifully with fish, particularly shellfish, as well as with other light white meats and anything curried. Although difficult to find, good Chenin is something worth seeking out!

Hip Tips
Chenin Blanc

- Chenin Blanc is also widely grown in South Africa, where it's often called "Steen."
- The best versions are from France's Loire Valley.
- It can be tough to find affordable, good quality Chenin Blanc, so consult a reliable wine merchant for help in tracking down the best bottlings.

Viognier
Status: Solo Star and Backup
Everyone, meet my favorite swinger. Viognier is one of those enviable grapes that produce wines that please white and red wine fans alike—a tough feat indeed. Because it's a full-bodied white wine, Viognier mimics some of the textural components found in rich red wines and, as a result, has been known to lure red wine–only types over to the light side of the wine divide.

Long known predominantly as an obscure blending grape in France's Rhône Valley, Viognier loves warm climates and produces heady, perfumed wines that are redolent of notes of peaches, baking spices, and flowers. It's stood on its own in the tiny French appellations of Condrieu and Château Grillet for many years, but only recently gained a foothold as a varietal wine stateside. Now, showy full-bodied whites made from this charming grape are popping up in warmer growing regions, namely along California's hot Central Coast and in South Africa.

Due to its characteristic high alcohol content (indeed, many Viogniers clock in above 14 percent alcohol) and low level of acidity, Viognier is not the most food-friendly wine on the market. However, it makes an ideal wine to order at a meal when a single wine will be consumed by many diners and with a variety of foods: It'll work tolerably with fish and white meats, while holding its own against rich dark meats and other hearty fare. It's also dynamite when sipped on its own, as a wine cocktail.

Hip Tips
Viognier

- Viognier is a rich white wine that's recently gained popularity in the United States. Watch for versions from California's Central Coast.
- Tough to partner with food due to its high alcohol and low acid, but makes an ideal cocktail wine or go-to selection for groups ordering mixed fare.
- Although gaining in popularity, Viognier can be tough to find on retail shelves. Still, the best merchants carry it, without a doubt.

Gewürztraminer
Status: Solo Star

And now: the spicy white. "Gewürz" literally means "spice" in German, and some of the better renderings of the grape do indeed show aromas and flavors of spice. However, more often wines made from this Germanic grape smell of roses and exotic fruits such as lychee. Personally, I've smelled only one intensely spicy Gewürz, as I like to abbreviate it, and it came from Australia's little-known wine region of Tasmania. But no matter what a Gewürztraminer smells like, this is for sure: It's incredibly aromatic!

Like other superaromatic whites, including Sauvignon

Blanc and Riesling, Gewürztraminer offers up a treasure trove of delights to the noses of tasters. Almost solely bottled on its own as a varietal wine, Gewürz has trademark floral and fruit notes that are hard to miss. It's most often bottled in dry or slightly sweet versions in France's Alsace and in some parts of California, although fully sweet dessert versions are also made in Alsace from grapes harvested late in the autumn. For these, watch for the words *vendange tardive* (late harvest) on the label.

Like Viognier, Gewürz can be perilously low in acidity, a condition that makes it difficult to pair with food. However, when produced in cool enough climates, Gewürztraminer packs adequate acid to partner beautifully with exotic foods, including Thai (especially when the wine is made in the slightly sweet style), and rich white meats like turkey. In fact, I think Gewürztraminer is the perfect white wine for Thanksgiving, since its rich body and moderate acid work well with the savory fare of the holiday table (think big: turkey, stuffing, and mashed potatoes).

Hip Tips
Gewürztraminer

- The best versions of Gewürz hail from France's easterly Alsace region. Your best bets are the bottles labeled "grand cru." Good Gewürz is also made in Tasmania, Washington, and Oregon.
- Gewürztraminer is the ultimate white wine for Thanksgiving, as its rich body and moderate acid partner well with turkey and its hefty sides.
- Late-harvest Gewürztraminer from Alsace is a super-sweet dessert wine that's perfect for apple tarts and pecan pie.

Pinot Gris/Grigio
Status: Solo Star
Pinot Gris is the Big Easy. Here's why: Pinot Gris (also Italy's Pinot Grigio) is remarkably easy to like, doesn't usu-

ally cost a lot, and partners well with a broad array of foods. You see: easy. Pinot Gris is a mutation of Pinot Noir; the name means "gray Pinot," and the grapes themselves are in fact rather pinkish-gray in color. The wine, however, is white, and the best versions hail from France's Alsace (yes, again!), northern Italy, and Oregon, and pack lots of crowd appeal.

In Oregon, Pinot Gris produces medium- to full-bodied wines with aromas of citrus fruits, apples, pears, peaches, and a hint of spice. Italian renderings are medium-bodied and often incorporate notes of mineral, tangerine, and flowers. I love good quality Italian Pinot Grigio because it's so versatile: It marries the qualities of crisp, food-friendly whites (Sauvignon Blanc and Riesling come to mind) with a bit more richness and body, which makes it appealing to folks who shy away from the mouth-puckeringly tart qualities of the most crisp white wines. But beware: Oceans of cheaply made Pinot Grigio have lately flooded the U.S. market, and these versions often bear little resemblance to the better stuff. (Giveaway: The cheaply made stuff usually comes in the bigger 1.5-liter bottles; avoid it!)

And finally, Pinot Gris from France's Alsace is the biggest-bodied rendering of the grape around, with the same citrus and apple-pear-peach qualities described above alongside a more pronounced spice note. This spiciness makes Gris great with rich white meats—think Thanksgiving fare, as with Gewürz—as well as spicy Indian foods and smoked cheeses. Reach for Gris when you're looking to try something new with a group—you'll be surprised at what a crowd-pleasing Big Easy it can be.

Hip Tips
Pinot Gris

- Called Pinot Grigio in Italy, Pinot Gris is a versatile white that pleases fans of lighter wines as well as those who look for more body in their glass.
- Gris smells of citrus fruits, apples, pears, peaches, and

spice, and partners well with rich white meats, smoked cheeses, and Indian fare.

- Avoid the mass-produced versions flooding the U.S. market; they bear little resemblance to the real thing.

Muscat
Status: Solo Star and Backup

It's true: I like to drink wine for breakfast. Moscato d'Asti, that is. Muscat is the beautifully perfumed white grape that appears in innumerable incarnations all over the world, although none is more famous than Italy's Moscato d'Asti. A light-bodied, fizzy delight, Moscato d'Asti is low in alcohol and almost too easy to quaff; hence its reputation as the ultimate breakfast wine. It smells of oranges, musk (literally, perfume), and honey, and is simply divine.

Muscat also appears in some dry versions—notably from France's Alsace—but most often we see it in sparkling and sweet forms. It's the main ingredient in many of the fabulously luscious *vins doux naturels* (VDN) dessert wines from France, and it also figures prominently in sweet sippers in most places where wine grapes grow. Some of the better-known versions are the insanely sweet Liqueur Muscats made in Australia, and California produces quite a few as well.

Muscat almost always smells of oranges and honey, and also has the remarkable distinction of being the only wine grape that makes wines that actually *smell* like grapes (as opposed to everything else under the sun). It's an ideal match with fresh fruit as well as fruit-based custards and tarts, and it's a classic match with chocolate, as the orange aromas and flavors found in Muscat seem to perfectly offset the deep richness of cacao. All in all, I've had many Muscats, some outstanding, some just adequate, but rarely have I not enjoyed myself.

Hip Tips
Muscat

- Wonderfully low-alcohol fizzing versions from Italy called Moscato d'Asti make the perfect breakfast wines.
- Full-bodied dessert wine versions of Muscat are made all over the world, but most notably in France and Australia.
- Muscat partners fabulously with fruit-based desserts and chocolate.

Grüner Veltliner
Status: Solo Star
Let's give it up for Grüner Veltliner, the weird-sounding wine for the chic wine geek in all of us. With its superlight body and crisp citrus notes backed by a lovely floral essence and surprisingly spicy note of white pepper, it's simply unique and makes the perfect white for salads and veggie dishes.

The darling grape of Austria, Grüner, as I like to call it, is so light in color you might mistake it for water. But water Grüner is certainly not. Instead, it's another "clean" white like Riesling, which doesn't see a dollop of new oak, and as such effortlessly transmits its crisp aromas and flavors to the palates of adventurous drinkers looking to try something different. Stylistically sandwiched between Riesling and Sauvignon Blanc, Grüner marries the lovely mineral and floral notes found in Riesling with the herbaceousness of Sauvignon, and to this it adds its own dash of pepper on the palate. Besides partnering well with salads and other green fare, Grüner works fantastically with herbed chicken and fish.

Since it's a rather obscure varietal, you're not going to find Grüner at every wine retailer, but it's popping up more and more on trendy wine lists across the land, as well as on the shelves of adventurous wine merchants.

- A quirky light-bodied white that's rapidly gaining steam among trendy sippers and sommeliers, Grüner is hard to find but worth the search.
- One of the few wines that works well with salads and other veggie fare, Grüner also partners well with fish and chicken.
- Grüner is to Austria what Riesling is to Germany: the main show.

Sémillon
Status: Backup

Sémillon is the rich, mouth-coating (sometimes even described as "oily") white from France's Bordeaux that's the key ingredient in the world-famous dessert wine Sauternes. Because Sémillon is thin-skinned, it's susceptible to a rare benign fungus called *Botrytis cinerea* that causes its clusters to shrivel into superconcentrated bunches that produce fabulously rich sweet wines. Appealingly referred to as the "noble rot," *Botrytis* happens when foggy mornings are followed by warm, sunny afternoons. Dessert wines made from grapes affected by it offer up luscious aromas of honey, apricots, flower blossoms, and ginger, and are considered the ideal accompaniments to superrich foie gras. Sémillon also shows up in dry white wines from Bordeaux and Australia, where a good amount of zippy Sauvignon Blanc lends crispness to this full-bodied white.

- The key ingredient in the luscious dessert wines of Sauternes, some of the world's most expensive wines and the ideal match for luxe foie gras.
- Sauternes is capable of aging for one hundred years or more!

Marsanne and Roussanne
Status: Solo Stars and Backup
Southern France's Rhône Valley is the ultimate stomping ground for blended wines, and Marsanne and Roussanne are king and queen, you might say, when it comes to whites that figure prominently in blends there. Along with aromatically assertive Viognier, Marsanne and Roussanne appear there in both white and red blends (although these grapes are decidedly white). Roussanne is the more elegant of the two, and its main responsibility is contributing its pretty aromas of lime blossoms and herbs to blends; Marsanne then lends weight and texture. Besides these roles, Marsanne and Roussanne have been known to show up from time to time as varietal wines in the United States and Australia.

Hip Tips
Marsanne and Roussanne

- Roussanne is one of four blending grapes allowed in rare white wines from France's famous region of Châteauneuf-du-Pape (the wines are called Châteauneuf-du-Pape Blanc).
- Good varietal versions of both are increasingly available from California's Rhône-like Central Coast.

A Few Good Whites

Here are the dets on a few other white wines worth knowing:

Muscadet. This fantastically light-bodied white from France's Loire Valley pairs high acidity with a pleasantly neutral flavor, making it the ideal accompaniment to the most briny and salty seafood, especially oysters.

Vermentino and Verdicchio. These refreshing Italian whites are great with food and make imaginative alternatives to the usual white wine suspects we sometimes tire of.

Sauvignon Blanc–like Vermentino is crisp and floral, while Verdicchio has a rounder, bigger body, with a surprising nutty finish that's unique.

Portuguese Vinho Verde. Literally, "green wine." Vinho Verde is a simple, supercrisp white wine that works well with salads and other veggie-laden fare.

Spanish Albariño. A white wine from Spain that marries sturdy acidity with its rather high alcohol. Quite trendy now, it's a versatile white that's sometimes oaked, sometimes not.

Onward

Now that you're well schooled in the world of whites, let's move on to the reds!

 All Aboard the Pinot Bus

Several years ago if you asked for "a glass of Pinot Noir" at your average restaurant you'd have been met with raised brows and an inquisitive look. Either the server wouldn't have known what Pinot was or he was so caught by surprise at your sophisticated, offbeat choice that it took him a minute to process it. Did this earthling really just order a glass of otherworldly Pinot? Today you're more likely to be asked in response, "Would you prefer a Pinot from California or France?" Or "We just got this awesome new one in from New Zealand. . . ."

Since the film *Sideways* catapulted the varietal to the forefront of America's wine consciousness a few years ago, you'll be hard-pressed to find folks who haven't heard that Pinot is considered the finicky favorite of the flick's main character, Miles. But what resonates with me more than the newfound popularity of my favorite red grape variety is the way that it's become a part of our pop culture fabric practically overnight. Thanks to a film, folks who've never before sampled wine have been turned on to the good stuff, and their enthusiasm is a big reason for Pinot's astronomical success in the past couple of years.

Even better news is that there are tons of other great red grapes out there besides Pinot, and getting to know them can be terrifically fun. Read on to get acquainted with the wine world's most popular red grapes and a handful of rising stars, because even cooler than asking for an esoteric Pinot at the wine bar is when you're also familiar with the likes of Pinotage, Primitivo, and Petite Sirah.

Chapter 4

It's a Red, Red World

Just like white grapes, red varieties run the gamut in terms of popularity and personality. Read on for an overview of the world's most popular reds, including Pinot Noir, Cabernet Sauvignon, and Syrah, as well as snapshots of lesser-known grapes worth seeking out. And who knows? You may even find a new favorite or two.

The Major Players

Pinot Noir: The Breakout Artist
Status: Solo Star and Backup
Pinot is rapidly gaining popularity in the United States, and its lovely light body, subtle red fruit, and spice qualities are showing newbie wine fans that there is indeed a yin to

the yang of high-octane, full-bodied reds like Australian Shiraz and California Zin. Not that there's anything wrong with the big guys, but Pinot is such a breath of fresh air on the red side of the wine scene that it's no mystery to me why it's flying off store shelves.

Burgundy: More Than Just a Shade of Red

Pinot's historic home is France's Burgundy, a smallish region not far from Dijon, where they make the mustard. In Burgundy you'll find only two key grapes growing: Chardonnay and Pinot Noir. Sounds easy to remember, right? Well, it is, but pretty much everything else about Burgundy is beyond complicated. Included in the principal area's approximately twenty-three thousand acres of vines are more than seventy subregions where wine is produced. Still more complex, many of these subregions are further subdivided into three quality levels: nondesignated (which means these bottles carry just the name of their subregion on them), *premier cru,* and *grand cru.*

This spells serious confusion for about 99.9 percent of the wine-drinking population, because—as you might imagine—it's beyond impractical to memorize all of these details. Further complicating things, because wines from Burgundy follow the place (versus the grape) format for naming, nowhere on the bottles from these subregions does it say "Chardonnay" or "Pinot Noir." Instead, the bottles simply list the name of the subregion from which the wine hails. Then it's up to you, savvy customer, to know that—*bien sûr*—a bottle labeled Vosne-Romanée or Musigny is really a Pinot! But some of the world's most delicious and complex Pinots hail from Burgundy, so it can pay to invest at least a little time in familiarizing yourself with some of the better subregions there. For this, flip to the Appendix for a list of Burgundy's best areas, broken out conveniently by value and quality.

The Bottom Line

Pinot Noir is fast gaining speed as the red grape of choice among both folks new to wine and connoisseurs (it's long been a favorite of collectors and sommeliers). Its lightness of body, soft tannin, and subtle flavors make it an ideal food wine, although it's more at home with rich white meats like veal and pork than with heartier steak and game. And Pinot takes well to oak, which is why you'll often find nuances of toast and baking spice in its mix, as well as a wonderful creaminess of texture. If wine could come out of my faucet, I'd be over the moon if it was Pinot.

When to Drink?

Lots of this has to do with where Pinot Noir is made. Versions from Burgundy's best vineyards can last up to fifteen or more years in a cellar; most made in California's warmer climate, on the other hand, are wonderfully drinkable right out of the door. Oregon also makes some very good Pinot Noir, too, and the stuff slides stylistically right in between those from Burgundy and California: It tends to be capable of longer-term aging, but are also ready to drink pretty much from the get-go. Newly hip New Zealand Pinot Noir, for the most part, is also one to drink soon after it's released.

Aromas and Flavors

Pinot's key aromas include red fruits like strawberries and cherries over a warm layer of characteristic earthiness. Notes of leather and spice also invariably creep in, the latter courtesy of the French oak barrels used for lots of the better versions of the stuff. Pinot Noirs hailing from warmer climates like California tend to be more fruit dominated, while those from France and, to a certain extent, Oregon often incorporate more noticeable nuances of earthiness in the mix. No matter where it's made, good Pinot Noir is smooth on the palate, thanks to its soft or "velvety" tannins, as they're often called.

Common Aromas

Red fruits: cherry, strawberry
Also: vanilla, caramel, smoke, earth, mushrooms,
    leather, game, spice, clove

Common Flavors

Red fruits: cherry, strawberry
Also: vanilla, caramel, smoke, earth, game, spice,
    pomegranate

Home Sweet Home

France: Burgundy, Alsace
California: Sonoma, Central Coast, Santa Barbara,
    Mendocino
Oregon
New Zealand

Blends: Watch for It In

Champagne

Merlot: The Misunderstood Misfit
Status: Solo Star and Backup
Fresh on the heels of our Pinot discussion is the perfect time to introduce Merlot. Sadly misunderstood, Merlot is currently suffering from a major PR crisis in the United States. There are a couple of reasons for this. For starters, *Sideways* didn't help. In the flick, curmudgeonly wine geek Miles's repeated bashing of the grape fueled a fire already smoldering among winos across our land. Their gripe? That Merlot is a flabby (read: critically low in acid)

red wine turned out by the overoaked boatload for consumption by ignorant quaffers who don't know any better.

Which brings us to the second reason for Merlot's current PR disaster: The "overoaked boatload" accusation is partly true. Merlot became an instant hit on the domestic wine scene in the midseventies after a guy named Louis Martini introduced it to the public in California as a varietal wine. Up until then it had been produced mostly in France as an anonymous partner in many Bordeaux blends, with the occasional starring role over there in reds from the appellations Pomerol and St.-Émilion. Merlot from this part of France is world-class stuff, but few people had any idea that it's what they were drinking when knocking back a six-hundred-dollar bottle of Château Cheval Blanc or Pétrus.

Back to the United States. Because Merlot is a low-acid grape, when grown in warm climates like some parts of California, it can produce wines that are indeed overly soft and even, well, flabby. These versions of Merlot (or any critically low-acid grape, for that matter) taste lousy with food and are uninspiring at best, impossible to drink at worst. As unscrupulous producers got wind of Merlot's growing popularity in the seventies they began turning out oceans of it made with subpar fruit that was then excessively doused with inexpensive sweet-smelling oak. By the nineties, the quality of most Merlot made in California had dropped so precipitously as to warrant its bad rap.

The Comeback

The bad rap is too bad, because when it's well made Merlot can actually be fantastic, and it can partner terrifically well with food (a good filet mignon comes to mind). The better versions of it don't deserve to be grouped with the oceans of flabby swill responsible for its crash-and-burn PR image. Fortunately, conscientious producers are scrambling to rectify Merlot's reputation stateside in the face of declining sales.

Merlot Fights Back

Swanson Vineyards, the single largest producer of estate-grown Merlot in Napa Valley, launched a nationwide campaign called Merlot Fights Back to reeducate the public about the merits of Merlot in the wake of *Sideways* and plummeting sales. Swanson winemaker Chris Phelps and general manager Stuart Harrison took to the road to show curious consumers that the varietal—contrary to its sullied reputation—figures in some of the most interesting wines from around the world. They continue their fight online at merlotfightsback .com, where they point out the ironic makeup of the '61 Château Cheval Blanc that the character Miles drank toward the end of the movie: It was a fifty-fifty blend of Cabernet Franc and—you guessed it—Merlot!

The Bottom Line

Choose wisely when it comes to Merlot. I like to stick to a handful of producers from California's Napa and Sonoma regions that I know and trust (see Appendix for a list), and excellent versions are coming from cool Washington State, where the crisp climate assures that the varietal nets adequate acidity to work with food. Wines from the Right Bank district of Bordeaux are great bets, but as with all Bordeaux, it pays to seek out versions from the better vintages. Again, peruse the vintage chart at the back of this book for guidance on purchasing. And finally, some very good Merlot can also be had from Chile.

When to Drink?

Good quality Merlot—the kind of stuff you ought to seek out—should be pleasant in the near term, although lots of it will improve with five to eight years in the bottle. Versions from the Merlot-centric St.-Émilion and Pomerol districts in Bordeaux are definitely worth looking for on restaurant lists, since you can usually drink them sooner than their Cabernet-driven counterparts from the rest of Bordeaux. Varietal versions hailing from Washington State and California, on the other hand, will be good within a year or two of release but may be even better after a few more years. Still: Proceed with caution, as there's lots of Merlot out there that's not good now, nor will it ever be.

Aromas and Flavors

Merlot can smell of many things, but it almost always incorporates aromas of plums and chocolate. The combination of these rich flavors, along with Merlot's signature low acidity, have frequently drawn comparisons to desserts like bread pudding, something I tend to agree with. Heartier renderings can take on more nuanced notes of spice, coffee, tobacco, herbs, and leaves. With age, good Merlot develops a lovely hazelnut aroma that I consider one of the most fabulous scents coming out of a glass.

Common Aromas

Red fruits: plum, cherry, strawberry
Also: chocolate, vanilla, cream, coffee, herbs, tea leaves

Common Flavors

Red fruits: plum, cherry, strawberry
Also: chocolate, vanilla, cream, coffee, herbs

Home Sweet Home

France: Bordeaux
California: Napa, Sonoma
Washington
Chile and Argentina

Much Ado About Meritage

Meritage—which rhymes with heritage—is the American-coined term for Bordeaux-style blends made outside of that great region. Because wines produced in the United States must be made up of at least 75 percent of a single grape variety in order to carry its name on the label, wines made of, say, 60 percent Cabernet Sauvignon and 40 percent Merlot (a typical Bordeaux blend) are ineligible for varietal labeling. These blends, therefore, usually go by proprietary names created by their producers. Popular Meritage reds including Opus One, Joseph Phelps Insignia, and St. Supéry Élu are made from two or more of the typical Bordeaux grapes—Cabernet Sauvignon, Merlot, Cabernet Franc, Petit Verdot, and Malbec—while Meritage whites are made from Sémillon and Sauvignon Blanc.

Blends: Watch for It In

Bordeaux, where it's the key ingredient in blends from the famous appellations Pomerol and St.-Émilion as well as in red blends from throughout the region
Meritage blends from California and similar bottlings from Washington State and Chile

Cabernet Sauvignon: The Power Grape
Status: Solo Star and Backup

When you think of fancy wine auctions—the kind that go down at tony places like Christie's and Sotheby's—it's usually Cabernet Sauvignon they're calling up to the block. Tannic, muscular, and capable of aging for decades or even up to a century in a cellar, Cabernet Sauvignon is *the* wine of collectors. The best versions come from Bordeaux (where it forms the backbone of most of that region's blends) and California's Napa Valley (where it shines on its own as a varietal wine), although, much like Chardonnay, it's also grown widely all over the world.

What's the big deal? you must be wondering. Well, if you've ever had a superbly aged version, you'll know. Good quality mature Cab is a beautifully smoky, nutty, and earthy thing that's worth traveling long distances and paying lots of money for. Seriously! Hence the auctions. Younger versions produced outside of Bordeaux, on the other hand, are really all about up-front fruit and grippy tannic structure, a combination that makes them ideal companions for consuming in the near term with red meat–driven dishes and other hearty fare.

A Question of Oak

If ever there was a wine destined for oak aging, it's Cabernet. The thick-skinned child of Sauvignon Blanc (yes, the white grape) and inky Cabernet Franc, Cabernet Sauvignon has a big structure that is well suited to the softening benefits of barrel aging. Over time oak imparts nuances of toast, smoke, hazelnut, and spice to a wine, a combination that's absolutely divine as the wine gets older.

The Bottom Line

Cabernet has long been the darling grape of Bordeaux, but in the last thirty years it's rapidly gained a foothold in other corners of the world. South Africa, Australia, Chile, and California are among the standouts, and versions from these areas can possess the winning combination of finesse and power that's the hallmark of the grape.

When to Drink?

New World–style Cabs—those from anywhere outside Bordeaux, for the most part—are rife with juicy fruit and possess softer tannin that usually makes them ready to drink just as soon as they're made. Versions from Bordeaux are different beasts entirely, and usually require years of mellowing in a cellar before their tannins soften to a state in which the stuff is actually drinkable. Because vintages vary greatly in Bordeaux, I highly recommend consulting the vintage chart at the back of this book for guidance in purchasing and drinking the stuff. When should you drink aged Bordeaux? When you're dining on an expense account, natch.

Aromas and Flavors

Cabernet is known for its distinctive black currant, tobacco, coffee, and mint notes. The oak chimes in next, with nuances of vanilla, toast, and spice. Finally, Cabernet is also capable of transmitting a good dose of a vine's *terroir*. In Napa's celebrated Rutherford district, for example, this comes across as dusty red fruit. Versions from Bordeaux also often include an undercurrent of pencil shavings or cedar wood.

Common Aromas

Red/dark fruits: black currants, blueberries, black plums
Also: spearmint, pencil shavings, cedar, toast, coffee, tobacco, dust

Common Flavors

Red/dark fruits: black currants, blueberries, black
  plums
Also: spearmint, coffee, licorice, bell pepper, tobacco

Home Sweet Home

France: Bordeaux
California: Napa, Sonoma, Santa Cruz
Argentina
Australia: Coonawarra, Barossa
South Africa

Blends: Watch for It In

Bordeaux, where it's the backbone of most red wines
Meritage blends from California
Australia, where it's often mixed with Shiraz and
  Grenache to form unique blends
Italy, where it's blended with Sangiovese in the
  faddish Super-Tuscans

Zinfandel: The Sunshine Grape
Status: Solo Star

Although it was long held that Zin is native to California,
recent research has shown that the grape is in fact the same
as southern Italy's Primitivo. But no matter: This new
knowledge hasn't dissuaded passionate California supporters
of the grape from attempting to pass legislation declaring it
the signature grape of the Golden State. Spicy, jammy, and
capable of producing wines of wildly varying intensity—
from elegant Pinot Noir–esque versions all the way up to
full-throttle tannic versions—Zin is a fascinating grape
that's an undisputed favorite among consumers, and a win-
ner with just about anything BBQ'd.

Zinfandel thrives in hot temperatures where its signa-

California

Mendocino

Sonoma

Napa

Sierra Foothills

Lodi

Santa Cruz
Mountains

Monterey

Paso Robles

Santa Barbara

Temecula

ture jammy fruit and pepper qualities reach their height. Key regions include California's roasting Central Coast and the similarly scorching inland area around the northern California town of Lodi. The most elegant renderings are produced in California's cooler Sonoma County from old vines that date back eighty years and more. Besides these table-wine versions, Zin also shows up in dessert wines from California, most of which are made from superripe late-harvested grapes.

Asphalt Never Tasted So Good

As I've mentioned before, one of my favorite things about wine is its ability to smell and taste like so many different things. Some of them, like Sauvignon Blanc's signature cat's pee aroma, sound downright bizarre—and I love that! Add Zinfandel to the list of wines with weird scents. In the case of Zin, that bizarre scent is tar. That's right, whether you refer to it as asphalt, pavement, or tar, it's definitely present in some of the best California Zins—especially those from the Central Coast's Paso Robles region—and it's something I find myself looking forward to every time I try a new Zin.

The Bottom Line

The darling of California, Zinfandel's never been grown with much success elsewhere. In the Golden State it creates reds of varying intensity that always carry signature jammy fruit and pepper notes that are perfect companions to casual foods and anything grilled. Very good versions can be had for under twenty dollars, so why pay more? Watch for versions from Paso Robles and Sonoma's Dry Creek Valley.

When to Drink?

Because Zin offers up superripe fruit from the day of its release, it's almost always best enjoyed right away. Another reason for this is the wine's moderate acidity: Even when Zin packs a solid tannic punch, the acid level rarely matches up, making it ill fit for the cellar. Instead, enjoy Zin for what it is: a *big* jammy red that's perfect for 'que and grilled foods right out the door. Plus, it's also dynamite with pizza, PB&J, and other foods that mimic its sweet jammy flavors.

Aromas and Flavors

Zin can taste of raspberry, blackberry, cherry, plum, and even strawberry preserves. The key here is fruit. After this, Zin almost always has an undercurrent of pepper running through it, and can also show hints of baking spices, herbs, licorice, tar, and smoke. It's this combination of lip-smacking sweetness and spiciness that makes folks fall in love with it time and again.

Common Aromas

Red/dark fruits: jammy blackberry and raspberry, cherry, plum
Also: tar, pepper, spice, herbs, licorice, cinnamon

Common Flavors

Red/dark fruits: jammy blackberry and raspberry, cherry, plum
Also: pepper, spice, herbs, licorice, cinnamon

Home Sweet Home

California: Paso Robles, Lodi, Livermore Valley, Sierra Nevada foothills, Sonoma

Blends: Watch for It In

Don't! It stands alone.

Syrah: The Meaty Red
Status: Solo Star and Backup

Known as Shiraz in Australia and South Africa, Syrah is a hearty black-skinned grape that produces powerful red wines with lots of juicy fruit. Besides this, Syrah grapes grown in ideal *terroir* develop a peppery deli meat essence that's unique to the grape. This is particularly the case for those grown in France's northern Rhône Valley, where the grape is at its most expressive. There the grape often adds to this meatiness a smokiness that translates to some serious power coming out of your glass. And, although I usually shy away from drawing comparisons to the sexes, I think in this case it's totally appropriate to call Syrah a masculine grape.

It's easy to like Syrah, especially when you take into account its unmistakable, unique personality. In New World wine regions, Syrah's fruit essence takes center stage, with smoky and meaty nuances settling into the background. In France's Rhône Valley, on the other hand, where the grape is in its *terroir* element (hot weather, lots of wind, marginal sandy soil), count on notes of pepper, meat, and smoke upstaging the fruit. When it *does* come through, the concentrated, even stewed fruit flavors are wonderfully lip-smacking. These are the classic Syrah renderings that set the pace for the rest of the winemaking world.

A Grape by Any Other Name

Shiraz is the capital of Fārs, a province of Iran, which is why many people believe Syrah originated in Persia. Still others counter that it must come from *Syra*cuse in Sicily. That it's now called Shiraz in Australia only further complicates the picture. But just about every aficionado you ask will agree that no matter where Syrah got its start, it's unmistakably at its best in France's Rhône Valley, where the appellations of Hermitage, Cornas, and Côte-Rôtie (literally, the roasted slope) turn out superconcentrated versions of the stuff that continue to improve for many years in the bottle. And most aficionados also now agree that the grape in all likelihood is native to the Rhône.

The Bottom Line

Syrah makes some of the most dynamic and deeply concentrated red wines available. I highly recommend seeking out classic versions from France's Rhône Valley in order to experience the grape's peppery meat quality at its most expressive. Outside of France, wines made from the grape take on more fruit-centric qualities, and many of them are absolutely delicious. Thanks to its juicy fruit and fascinating smoke, pepper, and meat notes, Syrah makes a fabulous companion to rustic, meat-driven dishes. By the same logic, avoid it with fish or anything light.

When to Drink?

Versions from France's top Syrah appellations (Hermitage, Cornas, and Côte-Rôtie) require at least five to eight years in the bottle before their burly tannic structure softens enough to be enjoyed. Those from nearby St.-Joseph and Crozes-Hermitage, also in the Rhône, are lighter in body and can usually be drunk after just three to five years. Anything from the New World—most notably Australia, South Africa, and the United States for Syrah—can be enjoyed pretty much right out of the gate, although versions from top producers can improve with some bottle age.

Rhone Ranger Roundup

The Rhone Rangers are a charismatic group of American winemakers who craft Rhône-inspired wines stateside. By means of an informative Web site (Rhonerangers.org) and well-attended consumer tasting events, the group educates consumers about the background and merits of the twenty-two Rhone Ranger grapes that figure prominently in their wines. It's been recognized as one of the most effective organizations dedicated to furthering consumers' knowledge of the wine industry at large as well as for the wines made by members.

Aromas and Flavors

A Syrah without a little pepper and meat just isn't a Syrah in my book. Watch for these aromas and flavors as well as stewed plums and other dark fruits, plus licorice, earth, and herbs.

Common Aromas

Red/dark fruits: stewed plum, blackberry
Also: pepper, licorice, spice, earth, jam, deli meats, tar, smoke

Common Flavors

Red/dark fruits: stewed plum, blackberry
Also: pepper, licorice, spice, jam, deli meats

Home Sweet Home

France: Hermitage, Cornas, Côte-Rôtie, Châteauneuf-du-Pape
Australia
South Africa
California: Santa Ynez Valley, Sonoma, Napa Valley, Santa Cruz Mountains, Central Coast

Blends: Watch for It In

The famous blended reds of France's southern Rhône
Valley, particularly from Châteauneuf-du-Pape
Some blends from Australia, particularly alongside
Cabernet Sauvignon

Other Red Players

Sangiovese
Status: Solo Star and Backup

Sangiovese is the star of Chianti, where it's blended with several other grapes to create the easy drinking—although highly
variable—red wines we often enjoy with Italian fare. Sangiovese Grosso, a souped-up version (read: a superior clone) of
the grape, plays a starring role in Brunello di Montalcino, the
fabulously layered wine from Tuscany that's become the new
"cult" red on the wine scene. And, when mixed with Cabernet
Sauvignon, Sangiovese translates to the faddish and sometimes
outstanding Super-Tuscans, big-bodied New World–style
reds that deftly match up Sangiovese's plush cherry fruit and
earthiness with Cab's firm structure and ability to age.

Sangiovese's stomping ground is almost singularly
Italy's central Tuscany, although it's also grown extensively
throughout the rest of Italy and in some parts of California.
Versions from California are rapidly improving, and ex-
periments with Super-Tuscan–style blends using Cabernet
Sauvignon are enjoying a good amount of success. Back in
Italy, a recent drop in the quality of Chianti is slowly being
rectified, although for the time being I highly recommend
sticking to versions labeled "Chianti Classico" and "Chianti Classico Riserva"—the highest quality levels—in order to avoid being disappointed.

The real story in Sangiovese is the fabulous Brunello di
Montalcino, or "Brunello," as it's often abbreviated. I like to
think of it as the Ferrari of Tuscany, a description I think
appropriate for this quintessential Italian grape. These
charmers are best drunk after five or more years, and show

lovely aromas of herbs, roses, cherries, and licorice. With bottles starting at around forty dollars, Brunello is definitely a splurge, but absolutely worth it for special occasions. For a little less dough, Vino Nobile di Montepulciano is another souped-up Sangiovese that packs some serious stuffing.

Hip Tips
Sangiovese

- The main ingredient in Chianti, a wine of varying quality from Italy's Tuscany.
- It has lately achieved new fame when blended with Cabernet Sauvignon in the faddish Super-Tuscans, produced in Italy and California.
- A superior clone of Sangiovese called Sangiovese Grosso is responsible for concentrated reds called Brunello di Montalcino. These wines are hot!

Tempranillo
Status: Solo Star and Backup
Tempranillo is *the* red grape of Spain, where it's the main ingredient in famous reds from the northerly regions of Rioja and Ribera del Duero. It also shows up as a blending grape in Portugal's mighty dessert wine, port, which is made from as few as six and sometimes as many as forty-eight grapes (talk about a serious blend!). Early ripening Tempranillo (*temprano* literally means "early") likes warm climates—hence its affinity for Spain—where it produces dark berries that lend muscle but not much in terms of aromatics to red wines. In other words, Tempranillo is a great source for structure in wines, but these wines usually need to be aromatically propped up by something else in order to take on anything resembling a unique scent personality.

So, enter oak. Especially in Rioja, Tempranillo-based blends take on the signature vanilla aromas of the American oak that's used frequently in Spain. Besides this, I usually detect notes of cola and Twizzlers in Rioja reds, but whether these can be attributed to the grape or the oak I'm not sure! Indeed, most wine scholars (the über-geeks of the wine world) agree that Tempranillo doesn't seem to have a clear aroma and taste profile of its own. However, unoaked versions from Spain's emerging Navarra offer an opportunity to sample the varietal sans wood interference, and in these I sometimes pick up aromas of tobacco, herbs, and earth. Again, the jury's out on whether this is the Tempranillo talking or something more specific to the region of Navarra (*terroir*).

Tempranillo-based reds from Rioja come in several quality levels—*crianza, reserva,* and *gran reserva*—each of which packs more complexity than the last. My favorite thing about these wines is that there are mandatory waiting periods before they can be released (based on the amount of time they spend in oak), which means that by the time they make it onto retail shelves they've got at least a few years of age on them—a rarity in today's rapid-release wine market. Pair up these straightforward, easy-drinking reds with tapas, Mexican food, chicken, pork, and game-based dishes for crowd-pleasing combinations.

Hip Tips
Tempranillo

- Forms the backbone of Spain's most famous reds, including those from Rioja and Ribera del Duero.
- Young unoaked versions from Spain's newly hip Navarra present great value.
- Some good varietal versions are being made in California.

Trentino-Alto Adige

Friuli-Venezia Giulia

Veneto

Piedmont

Italy

Tuscany

Umbria

Campania

Puglia

Sardinia

Sicily

Nebbiolo
Status: Solo Star

Nebbiolo is probably the least-known great wine grape in existence. In fact, the progeny of the best Nebbiolo, northern Italy's world famous Barolo, has been called "the wine of kings and the king of wines." Yet, unless you're already a wine buff or just happen to randomly know a lot about Italy, you've probably never heard of it. Allow me to enlighten you: Nebbiolo is the thick-skinned red grape that thrives amid the fog (*nebbia*) of Italy's most famous wine region, Piedmont. For you gourmands out there, Piedmont—situated in the northwestern part of the boot—is also responsible for producing some of the world's most sought-after truffles. You like this place already, right?

We can thank Nebbiolo for the great wines of Barolo and Barbaresco, the two villages within Piedmont where the fantastic wines by the same names are made. Barolo is an exotically perfumed red known for its layered aromas of roses, tar, tobacco, violets, prunes, and licorice. It's also famous for its huge tannic structure, something that necessitates at least eight to ten years of waiting (ideally, more) before a bottle of it can be enjoyed. This hefty structure is less imposing in versions from nearby Barbaresco, which have similar aromas and flavors and can be enjoyed sooner. Both wines are best drunk with the heartiest, richest fare from northern Italy.

Get Real

Barolo's high price tag (most bottles start at around forty dollars) and *long* waiting period before it can be enjoyed make it an impractical wine for all but the most patient and well-funded enthusiasts. As alternatives, look to Barbarescos from solid vintages—a trusted wine merchant can point you toward these—as well as wines made from the grape Barbera. Also grown in Piedmont, Barbera is a less "noble" grape—in fact, it's often called "the people's grape" in Italy—that still captures some of the quintessential earthiness and finesse of its more royal cohorts. And, since it's usually available for less than twenty dollars a bottle, Barbera makes a far more budget-savvy introduction to this great region.

Hip Tips
Nebbiolo

- The base of northern Italy's Barolo, the "wine of kings and the king of wines," a deep, earthy, and beautifully perfumed red meant for the cellar.
- Also makes Barbaresco, a more subdued brother to Barolo that can be enjoyed earlier.
- Barbera makes an affordable alternative to Nebbiolo for folks looking to sample Piedmont's wines; look for versions from the subregions of Alba and Asti.

Petite Sirah
Status: Solo Star

A full-bodied red that's well described as "full-throttle" by tasters, Petite Sirah makes big wines that are fruity, spicy, and tannic. In fact, there's really nothing petite about it! A direct descendant of Syrah and another grape called Peloursin that's native to France's Rhône Valley, Petite Sirah is grown almost singularly in California, where it reaches alcohol levels of dizzying heights in the hottest parts of the state, notably along the Central Coast. It boasts big flavors of dark fruits, including blueberries and blackberries, and, in its best renderings, has a distinctive char or campfire smoke aroma I find fascinating. For this reason, it's tops with BBQ fare.

Hip Tips
Petite Sirah

- DNA fingerprinting recently revealed it's the child of Syrah and Peloursin, grapes native to the Rhône Valley in France.
- Produces high-octane, inky-dark red wines mostly in

California, where they regularly clock in at 14 percent alcohol and above.

- Dark fruit and char notes make this red perfect for big BBQ fare.

Gamay
Status: Solo Star
Anyone who's had a friendly, lunch time–appropriate Beaujolais-Villages red will agree that this light-bodied and pleasant wine can be absolutely delightful. Gamay is *the* grape of France's Beaujolais region, an area that's gained renown over the past decade as the origin of Beaujolais Nouveau, the simple, fruity red that's released every fall just weeks after it's bottled. But Beaujolais Nouveau is more of a marketing phenomenon than a serious wine, which is a shame because it overshadows some more serious—and delicious—wines also made there. Versions from the ten best growing plots in Beaujolais—called *crus*—have much in common with good Pinot Noir, and are the best red wines for Thanksgiving turkey.

Hip Tips
Gamay

- There are three levels of quality in Beaujolais: regional wines (Beaujolais), village wines (Beaujolais-Villages), and the mighty *crus*.
- Those from the top tier bear the names of their sub-regions, or *crus,* on the labels; watch for those from Morgon, Fleurie, Moulin-à-Vent, and Brouilly.
- Reasonably priced between ten and twenty dollars a bottle, the *crus* represent serious value among crowd-pleasing reds—these are some of my favorite wines of all time.

Grenache
Status: Backup and Solo Star
Called Garnacha in Spain, Grenache is widely grown along the Mediterranean in that great land as well as in France. It's the key grape used in the wonderfully earthy and rich reds from France's Châteauneuf-du-Pape (which also incorporate a good amount of Syrah) and stands on its own in varietal bottlings in Australia. Some of the best versions from Down Under come from old vines that infuse the wines with layered personalities reminiscent of renderings from the better parts of France. These are tough to track down but worth the search. And, thanks to its naturally light color, Grenache also shows up in pink form—it is the favorite grape for rosés in France's pink-centric Provence. Count on aromas and flavors of stewed fruits, earth, and herbs.

Hip Tips
Grenache

- Grenache is blended with Tempranillo in Spain to produce the well-known reds of Rioja; it's also a key player in newly hip Priorat reds, also Spanish.
- Watch for it in the heady dessert wines called *vins doux naturels* (VDNs) in the south of France, where it's often matched up with aromatic Muscat.
- Grenache is the main ingredient in some of the best rosés from France and Spain.

Overextraction Explained

Extraction is a routine part of the winemaking process that's lately run amok. Because some foolish folks associate deep color (we're talking reds here) with quality, winemakers have taken to something called extended maceration in order to leach

out the maximum amount of color from fermenting grapes. Because maceration—the color-leaching
process—also leads to the extraction of tannin from
the skins and seeds of the grapes, when it's over-
done the wines turn out overly tannic and freak-
ishly out of balance. Even worse, these wines are
terrible with food.

Malbec
Status: Solo Star

Never before has a grape made such a dramatic transforma-
tion from little-known backup singer to multiplatinum solo
artist as Malbec did late in the last century. Long an obscure
blending partner in the great wines of Bordeaux—centered
on Cabernet Sauvignon and Merlot—Malbec found its
own expression in the baking hot vineyards of Argentina,
where it's now the country's number one varietal red.
Deeply concentrated in both color and flavor (some Argen-
tine Malbecs are appropriately described as "syrupy"), Malbec is a giant red that is silky and rich and teeming with
flavors of red and black fruit. It's the perfect wine for today's
juicy fruit–loving palate.

Hip Tips
Malbec

- Tremendously successful in Argentina, where it's well
  matched by that country's *carne*-driven cuisine. The
  best steak fajita wine, hands down.
- Also makes rustic, little-known varietal reds in
  France's Cahors region.
- Although rich and lush, Malbec can also be perilously low in acidity, so avoid pairing it with anything
  too spicy or fatty.

A Few Good Reds

Here's some 411 on a few more reds worth knowing:

Nero d'Avola. Named for the town of Avola in the southern part of the island of Sicily (Italy), Nero d'Avola is a rich grape that makes full-bodied red wines with a pleasant undercurrent of herbs and spice.

Cabernet Franc. The principal blending partner of Merlot in Bordeaux's St.-Émilion and Pomerol districts, Cabernet Franc appears on its own in varietal wines from France's Loire Valley that are among the best reds for food. Watch for versions from the districts of Chinon and Bourgueil.

Pinotage. A cross between Pinot Noir and the inky-black Cinsault, Pinotage was literally created in a laboratory by a South African scientist with an oenological bent. Like a full-bodied, super-earthy Pinot Noir, Pinotage is essentially fruit-forward with some interesting chocolate notes in the background.

And Now, the *Really* Good Stuff

Whew! I'm glad you're still with me. Now that we've cased the world of grapes, it's time to get acquainted with two of my all-time favorite styles of wine—sparklers and sweeties.

From Bartles & Jaymes to Bollinger

I readily admit to having knocked back a few wine coolers in my early days of wine consumption. Sure, the fruity sparkling "wines" were hardly sophisticated, but then again being sophisticated isn't really the point at a keg party.

Now that I know a bit more about wine, I'm much more likely to pick up my sparkling wine from a reliable wine merchant than from the 7-Eleven, and it's also more likely bottled by the likes of Bollinger than by Bartles & Jaymes. But one thing that *hasn't* changed since those early days of wine experimentation is my unabashed enthusiasm for sparkling and sweet wines. Because no matter what the quality of the wine or the occasion, there's something undeniably exciting about popping the cork on a bottle of bubbly or opening up a delicious bottle of sweet stuff.

These are the wines we enjoy at special moments, on holidays, and when we feel like it's okay to splurge. That was the case back when the occasion was a Friday-night

kegger, and it's still the case when it's something more momentous, like your best friend's wedding or the birth of a
child. Only these days, instead of unscrewing the cap on a
wine cooler you're probably popping the cork on something a little more grown-up, like Veuve Clicquot Yellow
Label. Change, after all, can be a *very* good thing.

Chapter 5

Bubbly Basics and Sweet Treats

Champagne: A Reputation Well Earned

Champagne stands head and shoulders above the rest of the wine-producing world when it comes to fame. And for good reason: Besides being terrifically difficult to make and, at the higher end, incredibly expensive, Champagne is absolutely delicious stuff. No other wine can boast the crispness of acidity, layered flavors, and full body of really well-made Champagne. These qualities also explain why Champagne is hands down the best wine to pair with food—period.

And although it usually costs an arm and a leg, you'll be hard pressed to find anyone who doesn't treat herself to a bottle of this decadent stuff at least on her birthday or at New Year's—it's indisputably *the* wine of celebration and the good life. To that end, the best Champagne producers enjoy worldwide renown, a fact nowhere better evinced than among today's rappers, who have a penchant for superluxe bubbles. Surely, Champagne is the only wine that doubles a pop-culture phenomenon!

Capturing the Sparkle

There are, as you might imagine, lots of ways to get bubbles into liquid. Think about all the things we drink that have bubbles: soda, beer, energy drinks, mineral water, wine. Methods vary tremendously, but none is more time consuming and labor intensive than the traditional method used to make Champagne sparkle.

The French put it best when they said of Champagne production that what they're really doing is "capturing the sparkle." *La prise de mousse* is how they put it. Unlike other, mostly inexpensive, ways of making things bubbly—which usually involve the thrifty bicycle pump method (essentially pumping carbon dioxide gas into still liquid)—Champagne produces the bubbles *on its own* before they're harnessed and sealed up in the bottle by producers for our later enjoyment. You see: In this way they are *captured* rather than *created*.

How does this happen? Champagne goes through something called a secondary fermentation inside the bottle from which we eventually drink it. This process at first happened by accident, when still (read: nonbubbly) wines made in France's cool Champagne district were shipped in barrels over the English Channel to Britain. By a happy accident, the wine started *spontaneously refermenting* (no doubt due to residual sugar left in the juice and the presence of natural yeasts in the barrels) en route, giving off CO_2 in the form of bubbles. The Brits liked the result so much they started requesting more wine in the same style.

And, just like that, an industry was born.

Traditional Method (a.k.a. *Méthode Champenoise*) 411

The Champenois—as we refer to the residents of the famous region situated about ninety miles northeast of Paris—began replicating this second fermentation on their own by bottling their wines along with a small amount of sweet unfermented wine and yeast. This mixture of sugar and yeast, called *liqueur de tirage*, catalyzes a second fermentation postbottling, and the CO_2 that's a natural by-product of fermentation takes the form of bubbles that are trapped inside the bottle. We call it a second fermentation because the wine that's put into bottles has already undergone its primary, or alcoholic, fermentation in tanks. The second fermentation just serves to put the bubbles inside.

Make Mine a Mini

Savvy sparkling producers are responding to consumers' growing appreciation of so-called small format bottlings of the good stuff. For times when you'd rather not pop the cork on a full bottle of bubbly but still want to treat yourself to a nice glass of the stuff, reach for one of these convenient single serving–sized bottlings: POP by Pommery Champagne; Heidsieck & Co. Monopole's Little Blue Top; White Star from Moët & Chandon; Sofia Blanc de Blancs by California's Coppola; Segura Viudas Brut Reserva Cava from Spain; and Cristalino Brut Cava, also from Spain.

The used-up yeast cells, called lees, from the *liqueur de tirage* are then allowed to hang out in the bottle for as few as fifteen months for the most "generic" (if such a term can be used to describe Champagne!) bottlings and up to three years and sometimes more for the most prestigious ones. Over time the lees contribute a toasty creaminess to the wine that is quintessentially Champagne. When it's finally time to send the wine out into the world, the yeast cells are ejected from the bottles, which are then topped up and resealed. At this point all they need is a label and these beauties are ready for good people like you and me to enjoy.

Champagne Producers: Top Dogs

Global Champagne sales are dominated by a handful of the most powerful Champagne "houses," as they're often called. Their widely available sparklers vary in style, so I've listed a few of my favorites along with a brief description of what you can expect next time you have the good fortune to pop the cork on one of these. (Note that the descriptions apply to the houses' non-vintage bottlings.)

Laurent-Perrier—light and elegant, with notes of cream and fresh fruit.
Taittinger—light and elegant, with floral nuances.
Moët & Chandon—medium-bodied, with toast and floral notes.
Veuve Clicquot—medium-bodied, with biscuit and pear notes.
Charles Heidsieck—medium-bodied, with vanilla and toast.
Bollinger—full-bodied, with crisp fruit and nutty aromas.
Krug—full-bodied, with exotic fruit and toasty oak.

It's in the Blend

Virtually all Champagne is made of a blend of three different grapes: Chardonnay, Pinot Noir, and Pinot Meunier. The latter two are red grapes, but because their juice is pressed off of their dark skins immediately after picking, they produce clear juice. In the blend Chardonnay contributes elegance and finesse, Pinot Noir contributes structure and depth, and Pinot Meunier imparts richness and fruitiness. Individually they would produce still interesting but more singular wines; together they produce the unique combination of all these attributes that is Champagne's signature.

All in a Name

Because of strict regulations in the European Union, only bubblies made in the actual district of Champagne in France are supposed to call themselves by the name "Champagne." Pay close attention to any other sparkling wine from the EU, and you won't see the word "Champagne" anywhere on the bottle. To do so might bring a lawsuit from the Champenois—they're that serious about their brand! Because these laws don't apply outside of the EU, some bubblies made in other parts of the world still call themselves Champagne, much to the dismay of the makers of the real thing. Nonetheless, worldwide demand for Champagne is so great that every last bit of cultivable land in the approximately eighty-five-thousand-acre district of Champagne has been planted. This demand is great news for the Champenois but means ever-increasing prices for consumers.

Champagne Styles

Non-vintage. Besides being a blend of several different grapes, most Champagne is a blend of juice from several years' harvests. Dubbed non-vintage Champagne, wines made in this style make up the majority of Champagne produced every year, and this is the stuff we're used to seeing most often. Look closely and you'll see that these bottles don't bear a vintage year (e.g., 2005) anywhere on the label, due to the fact that they're almost always made from at least two years' juice, and sometimes many more.

In terms of style, the goal when it comes to non-vintage Champagne is that every year the new wines produced should taste exactly the same as those from the previous year, the year before that, and so forth. This process is achieved by a master blender or team of master blenders at each Champagne house. These folks' job, in a nutshell, is to create a consistent style from year to year, so that every time you pick up a bottle of Moët & Chandon White Star, for example, it tastes just like the last bottle of White Star you had. Tough job, eh? Expect to pay twenty-five dollars a bottle and up for non-vintage Champagne.

Recent Top Vintage Years in Champagne

1982
1988
1990
1995
1996
1998

Vintage. Besides their non-vintage bottlings, most Champagne producers also make something called vintage Champagne. Made only three or four times a decade in the very best years, vintage Champagne is produced when grapes from a single year's harvest are declared ripe enough to be bottled on their own (as opposed to blended with juice from other years).

This brings up another key point about the region of Champagne. Because it's situated at the far northern part of the wine-friendly band of the northern hemisphere—indeed, at 49.19° north latitude it's just shy of the upper limit of 50°—the weather there is highly variable from year to year. In some years the grapes just don't ripen enough to produce juice that can stand on its own as a vintage wine; hence the region's tradition of blending from several different years' harvests. Wines from ripe vintages mellow out the thin, acidic juice from less ripe years, re-sulting in the harmonious whole that is well-blended non-vintage Champagne.

Back to the vintage stuff. When a single year's weather is warm enough to allow the grapes to ripen adequately, Champagne houses may declare a vintage year and bottle some of the juice from that year on its own. These wines are meant—unlike the non-vintage stuff, which should al-ways taste the same—to reflect the nuances and idiosyn-crasies of that particular vintage year. So, from a region that's built its reputation on consistency with its non-vintage wines also come individualistic vintage bottlings several times a decade, if we're lucky. These special bottlings reflect their unique status on the price tag; expect to pay fifty dollars and up for them.

Top Prestige Cuvées

Perrier-Jouët (Belle Époque)
Moët & Chandon (Dom Pérignon)
Veuve Clicquot (La Grande Dame)
Louis Roederer (Cristal)

> Billecart-Salmon (Cuvée NF Billecart)
> Piper-Heidsieck (Rare)
> Laurent-Perrier (Grand Siècle)
> Pol Roger (Cuvée Sir Winston Churchill)
> Pommery (Cuvée Louise)

Prestige Cuvées. For those of you waiting with bated breath for the Cris and the Dom to come into play, now's your time. Besides producing vintage bottlings, the top Champagne producers also make something called luxury or prestige cuvées, which are, to borrow a page from the fashion industry, the haute couture of the wine world. For Louis Roederer this is Cristal, for Moët & Chandon it's Dom Pérignon, and for Veuve Clicquot it's La Grande Dame. These rare bottles can be tough to track down, but once you do they're capable of developing beautifully nuanced flavors in a cellar—if you can hold on to them for that long. Pick up a prestige cuvée for the really *big* occasions in life: graduations, engagements, weddings, anniversaries, and the like. They start at about one hundred dollars a bottle.

In Other Champagne News: Color and Sweetness

Blanc de Blancs. Champagne made entirely from Chardonnay grapes is called *blanc de blancs* ("white of whites"). These wines tend to be light in body and elegant in style, although some such as Salon's very rare Le Mesnil bottling require several years' worth of time for their assertive acidity to mellow.

Blanc de Noirs. Literally meaning "white of blacks," this is the French term for Champagne made exclusively from Pinot Noir and Pinot Meunier grapes. The juice is pressed quickly and gently off the skins of the dark grapes in order to preserve its lightness of color (hence, *white* of blacks), although many of the wines still carry a hint of pink color. *Blanc de noirs* bubblies tend to be more aromatic and rich than *blanc de blancs* versions.

Rosé. In Champagne production this indicates a bubbly made pink either by the *saignée* (bled) method or by adding a bit of dark wine to a white base wine. More fully pink than *blanc de noirs* versions, rosé Champagne is a fun twist on an already exciting drink. Nothing fits the bill better for Valentine's Day and other romantic occasions than pink Champagne.

How Sweet Are You?

Besides its various color incarnations, Champagne comes in a variety of sweetness levels. The signature sweetness style of Champagne is brut, or dry, but there are numerous variations on this theme, heading all the way up to fully sweet. Here's the 411 on the various levels, some of which sound downright confusing:

Extra Brut, or Brut Nature. As its name implies, extra or *very* dry.

Brut. This is what we see most often. Although "brut" literally means "dry" in French, there is actually a small amount of sugar in these wines; however, it's essentially imperceptible.

Extra Dry. Still more confusing, this is actually a step up in sweetness from brut; these wines are just perceptibly sweet.

Sec. A synonym for "dry" in French. Champagne bottles bearing sec on the label are actually somewhat sweet.

Demi-sec. "Half dry," although we're better off interpreting it as "half sweet." These are very definitely sweet wines that are ideal for cheese platters and fruit-based desserts.

Doux. Finally, a description that fits the bill! "Doux" means "sweet" in French, and that's exactly what sparkling wines bearing this description are.

For Best Bubble Performance, Towel Off Your Glass

Researchers recently discovered that hollow cellulose fibers such as those found on towels and clothing create bubble formation, or "nucleation," sites that stimulate effervescence in Champagne. Apparently, the CO_2 responsible for the bubbles in sparkling wine is catalyzed by the gas pockets lurking inside these cellulose fibers. The more fibers in your flute, the more animated your bubbly show once you pour in some of the good stuff. So, before pouring a glass of bubbly it's a good idea to towel off the inside of your flute to deposit some extra fibers for your bubbles to rally around. Then, sit back and enjoy the show.

Bubble Breakdown

Another thing that sets Champagne apart from its bubbly peers is the fineness and liveliness of its bubbles. The secondary fermentation that occurs inside the bottle during Champagne production translates to superfine (read: tiny) bubbles that stream animatedly upward in your glass long after you've poured the stuff in. Compare the bubbles of any Champagne with those of a lesser bubbly (i.e., one that has not undergone a secondary fermentation inside the bottle, like Champagne) and you'll note that those of the non-Champagne are bigger in size and die off quickly after pouring.

Why? Because other methods of sparkling-wine production just don't translate to the same degree of fineness and animation of bubbles. These other production methods include the industrial "bicycle pump" method whereby CO_2 gas is literally pumped into the liquid (this is the same method used for getting the bubbles into your run-of-the-mill soda). There's also an intermediate process called the tank, or Charmat, method that encourages a secondary fermentation inside a tank, after which the wine is bottled under pressure. This happy medium manages to capture more fine bubbles than the pump method, although it still can't rival Champagne's superior results.

Other Bubbly Stars

Champagne Look-alikes

As I mentioned earlier, bubblies from outside Champagne made in the traditional method "discovered" by the Champenois can't bear the name Champagne. (Although this is only regulated in the European Union, conscientious producers from around the world have begun omitting the term from their labels too as a courtesy.) Let's take a closer look at these Champagne look-alikes and what they call themselves.

Crémant. This is what we call traditional method sparkling wine made in France outside the Champagne region. Besides listing the term "Crémant" on the label, these wines also indicate the name of the subregion from which they hail. For example, versions from Alsace are called "Crémant d'Alsace," while those from the Loire Valley are dubbed "Crémant de Loire." Several other subregions produce Crémants, including Burgundy and Limoux, two of my favorites. Crémant wines are known for their wonderfully creamy mousse, or fizz, and make dynamite stand-ins for Champagne for about half the price.

Cava. Bubblies made in the traditional method in Spain's northeasterly Catalonia region bear the name "Cava" on their labels. These crisp, floral sparklers lack the steely acidity of Champagne but make up for it in their easy-to-appreciate price (they start at around six bucks a bottle) and softer, more fruity style. I like versions from Segura Viudas, a reliable producer that makes several different widely available cuvées, and Freixenet, a huge producer whose trademark black bottles contain pleasant, slightly sweet bubbly that's great for parties and big groups.

Synonyms for Méthode Champenoise

There are lots of ways to say *méthode champenoise,* the method of bubbly production that includes a second fermentation inside the bottle. For bubblies made in the Champagne style, watch for the following indications on the bottle:

Traditional method (English-language countries)
Méthode traditionnelle and *méthode classique*
    (France)
Crémant (France)
Cava (Spain)
Metodo classico and Talento (Italy)
Flaschengärung nach dem Traditionellen
    Verfahren (Germany)
Cap Classique (South Africa)

Sparkling Wine. While sparkling wines are made all over the world, the best sparklers outside of France come from California, in my opinion. A number of top Champagne producers seem to agree, as several of them have set up sister operations in the Golden State, where they're bottling Champagne-style bubblies that usually bear the indication "sparkling wine" on the label. These wines, especially versions from northern California's cool Mendocino County, combine the steely acidity of good bubbly with the finesse that comes from stellar production methods.

Watch for versions from Roederer Estate (Champagne Louis Roederer's Cali outfit), Domaine Chandon (ditto from Champagne's Moët & Chandon), and Schramsberg. Besides those from California, some very good traditional method sparkling wines are also made in Washington State, New Mexico, South America, and Tasmania.

Other Sparklers

Moscato d'Asti. This gloriously light-bodied Italian sparkler smells like oranges, musk, and flowers, and it's hands down the *best* wine to serve with breakfast. Why? Mostly because it's low in alcohol: Versions usually clock in at just 5.5 percent alcohol, a little more than in your typical beer. Besides this, Moscato's got low-intensity fizz (it packs only about half the fizz intensity of normal bubbly) and its subtle sweetness is deftly balanced by a zippy kick of acidity, making it one of the most refreshing wines around. Match it up with fruit-based desserts, anything breakfast-oriented (why not!?), or just sip it by itself after a long day. You'll feel better instantly, I promise. Watch for versions from Braida and Vietti.

Other Ways to Say "Bubbly"

As is the case for *méthode champenoise,* there are lots of other ways to describe sparkling wine. Here are a few other ways to indicate that a wine is sparkling in other countries. Note that terms are listed in order of increasing bubble intensity when multiple listings appear per country:

Frizzante, spumante (Italy)
Espumoso (Spain)
Sekt (Germany and Austria)

Prosecco. From northeastern Italy's Veneto region (as in close to Venice) comes a wonderfully approachable sparkling wine made from the Prosecco grape. The best versions of this fruity, sometimes slightly sweet white sparkler are made in the regions of Valdobbiadene and Conegliano, and will indicate as much on the label. Styles can vary widely, from completely dry versions up to fully sweet renderings, so be advised that you may be in for a surprise in terms of sweetness level (although some of the driest versions list "extra dry" or "extra brut" on the label). These are simple wines meant to be enjoyed on picnics and with fresh, uncomplicated fare like appetizers and antipasto. Reliable producers of these melony, floral bubblies include Aneri, Mionetto, and Zardetto.

Sekt. These are mostly mass-produced, simple sparkling wines from Germany and Austria. The best versions are called *Deutscher Sekt* and are made from Riesling, the darling grape of the Germanic countries. These can be light-bodied, prettily perfumed, and elegant, even approaching the quality of some of the better sparkling wines from around the world. Unlike the industrially produced basic *Sekt, Deutscher Sekt* will usually include the name of its subregion, vintage, and grape variety on the label.

Sparkling Sake. This relative newcomer on the domestic wine scene (the first bottles of sparkling sake trickled into the United States just a few years ago) is currently making a big splash among the lucky few who've tried it. Like Champagne, sparkling sake undergoes a secondary fermentation inside the bottle, which makes it lightly fizzy. It clocks in at just about 5 percent alcohol and boasts delicate floral aromas and a light sweetness that's just the right thing with triple cream cheeses, lightly spiced cuisine, and of course sushi. I like to think of sparkling sake, with its low alcohol and undeniably appealing fruit flavors, as the wine cooler of the new millennium.

Sparkling Shiraz. Made in Australia from the über-popular Shiraz grape, these ruby red sparklers are generally a little sweet, low in acid, and always lushly fruity. Uncomplicated, in other words. Better yet, some of them pack extra complexity in the form of the signature savory and pepper notes typical of the Syrah grape. All this, and you can't beat the "wow" factor of the color (when was the last time you had a *red* sparkling wine?!). Sparkling Shiraz pairs up beautifully with some of our favorite casual foods, including BBQ, which is why it's an ideal sparkler to reach for when you're heading to a potluck, picnic, or tailgate. Watch for widely available versions from Hardys, as well as those from Fox Creek, which are a little tougher to track down but worth the search.

Other Red Sparklers. If you like the idea of a crowd-pleasing sparkling Shiraz, you might consider two other deeply hued bubblies, both of which hail from Italy. Lambrusco is a popular lightly fizzing red produced in central Italy that first took the U.S. market by storm back in the eighties. It's usually slightly sweet, and wonderfully easy to drink, and it goes famously with cold meats and charcuterie. Brachetto d'Acqui is a fabulously aromatic medium-sweet sparkler produced in Italy's northeasterly Piedmont region, also home to Barolo and Barbaresco. One of my all-time favorite wines, Brachetto d'Acqui tastes like strawberries and pairs terrifically with chocolate- and fruit-based desserts. Yum.

Speaking of sweet wines, it's time to move on to our discussion of sweet treats!

Sweet Wines—with Respect

Sweet wines are a great mystery to most people. This is partly due to their rarity and partly due to the fact that most sweet wines that folks encounter during their early days of drinking are, well, crap. After the occasional brush with a cheap, sweetened jug wine, most folks decide that dry wines must be where it's at.

This is too bad, because the best sweet wines *of good quality* are some of the most fabulous things we can quaff and are capable of elevating your average run-of-the-mill dessert to dizzying heights of deliciousness, and your mood along with it. Great sweet wines are also the best partners to cheese trays (incomprehensible as it sounds) and can even be dynamite when sipped before a meal, as an aperitif. So, now that you know that there *are* great treasures to be found among the sweet wine ranks, let's take a closer look at these misunderstood vinous misfits.

The Rotten Wines

Contrary to the way it may sound, these sweet wines aren't naughty in any way, unless you consider being wickedly good an offense. "Rotten" is just my favorite way of describing wines that are made from the benevolent fungus *Botrytis cinerea* (also known as "the noble rot"). In certain very specific conditions—early morning fog followed by late afternoon sunshine, to be precise—the noble rot will attack grapes and shrivel them into superconcentrated nuggets that produce deliciously sweet wines.

Why? Because the fungus effectively dries the grapes out, removing much of their water but leaving behind their natural plant sugar. The resulting juice, of which there is much less, as you might imagine (hence these wines' hefty price tag), is supersweet, and makes some of the most unctuous dessert wines on the planet. Some of the best versions come from the subregions of Sauternes and Barsac in Bordeaux; some delicious ones are also made in Germany, Hungary, and a few other pockets of the world. Another reason for these wines' rarity is that the noble rot works its benevolent magic on only a few grape varieties— Bordeaux's Sémillon and Germany's Riesling chief among them. For most other grapes, the *Botrytis* fungus stops being noble and starts being a serious pest: You usually have to throw out these other *truly* rotten grapes.

Taste and Flavor Profile

Wines made from nobly rotten grapes are extremely sweet to the taste, with a deep golden honey color. As they age they turn even darker, so that very old versions can be nearly brown to the eye. Key aromas include honey, blossoms, apricots and peaches, figs, honeysuckle, and citrus peel. These are ideal wines for cheese trays (Sauternes and blue cheese make a great wine and food match) and most desserts, especially crème brûlée. Expect to pay at least thirty dollars a bottle, and way, way up.

The Frozen Wines

Okay, so these wines aren't literally frozen—they're just made from frozen grapes—but I love calling them "frozen" because it catches folks' attention as no other descriptor can. Unlike rotten wines, which become sweet when the fungus *Botrytis* dries them up and leaves their sugar behind, frozen wines develop superconcentrated sugars courtesy of the cold. More specifically, when grapes are allowed to stay on their vines late into the cool months—usually January in the northern hemisphere—they freeze, as you might imagine. (The same effect can be achieved by tossing grapes into a freezer, incidentally.)

When these grapes are pressed, much of their moisture, in the form of water crystals, gets caught in the press, and only a very small amount of high-sugar-content juice (which freezes at a lower temperature than water) runs through. And while it's a different process from the one for rotten wines, it has the same result: more sugar, less water in the juice. The name for wine made in this fashion is ice wine, although it appears variously as "Eiswein" on German labels and "Icewine" on Canadian bottlings. Chilly Canada produces by far the most ice wine in the world, although Germany has traditionally produced quite a bit as well. Increasingly, winemakers in the northern U.S. states of Oregon and Michigan are trying their hand at the stuff as well.

Taste and Flavor Profile

Ice wine is rapidly gaining in popularity in the United States, a fact that's music to my ears, since it's one of the most versatile dessert wines around. Besides working beautifully with cheese trays, like *Botrytis*-affected wines, ice wine is delicious with chocolate, fruit-based desserts, and even creamy desserts to boot. Gold in color, ice wine offers aromas and flavors of tropical, tree, and citrus fruits (e.g., mango, pear, and lime), baking spices, honey, and flowers. This is all balanced by wonderfully crisp acidity courtesy of the cool climates from which ice wines hail, making wines that balance their sweetness with a refreshing dash of zip. Plan on paying fifty dollars and up a bottle for these divine treats.

The End of Ice Wine Production?

The wine industry is all atwitter with scorching news about the worsening issue of global warming. Because climate plays such a key role in wine production, even the small shifts in temperatures we're observing all over the world due to global warming are having a major impact. Nowhere was this more clear than in Germany in January 2007, when the typically cool weather there failed to get chilly enough to make ice wine. As the world gets warmer, will winemakers find new, chillier stomping grounds for ice wine production? Stay tuned.

The Dried Wines

Now that we know that dessert wines can be made by rotting and freezing methods, it shouldn't come as a surprise that they can also be made by a drying process. Effectively, all of these processes (rotting, freezing, and drying—all very sexy sounding, I know) serve to dehydrate grapes, the result of which is that we get juice that's superhigh in sugar content, since any excess water has been removed. Wine-inclined folks have known about this happy result of dehydrating grapes for thousands of years, which is why dried wines, our next subject, have been around for about that long. Back in the day, the Greeks and Romans dried grapes in the hot Mediterranean sun to make megasweet amber-colored wines that were, in all likelihood, surprisingly similar to the dried wines we enjoy today.

The best example of this ancient technique is Italy's Vin Santo (literally, "holy wine"), which is the pride and joy of folks in sunny Tuscany, where they often hang bunches of grapes from the rafters to dry. After pressing and fermentation, Vin Santo wines are then aged for at least three and sometimes as many as ten or more years in oak, where they develop their lovely deep color and nutty nuances. Dried wines are also made in other parts of the world, including the south of France, Spain, and anywhere there's adequate heat and a hankering for the good stuff. In Italy's northeasterly Veneto, some red and white sweet wines are also made from dried grapes and sell by the names Recioto della Valpolicella and Recioto di Soave. Dried wines may also be referred to as "straw wine" or *passito*, the Italian word for "dried grape wine."

Taste and Flavor Profile

Styles of Vin Santo can vary widely, from supersweet versions to something that's much closer in style to a dry wine, but the aromas and flavors of these beauties are always unique. Expect notes of caramel, nuts, raisins, apricots, and figs. Vin Santo is dynamite with chocolate, biscotti, nutty desserts, and, for the drier versions, cheese and nut platters. Thirty dollars and up.

The Strong Wines

Besides the delicious—if unsexily named—sweet wines described above, there are a host of others that pack an extra alcoholic punch alongside their sweetness. These are the so-called fortified wines, or "strong wines," to which neutral spirit (read: booze, as in a flavorless brandy) has been added to achieve two tasks. Those are:

- To arrest fermentation, so that some of the sugar will remain in the wine rather than being entirely converted into alcohol (i.e., so the wine will be sweet!), and

- To bolster the finished wine—to make it stronger—with the additional alcoholic strength that comes from the booze. These wines are usually between 16 and 20 percent alcohol (compared with about 12 or 13 percent for most table wines).

Port: The Old Standby

The most classic example of a fortified wine is port. A strong, sweet wine that's long been associated with the British, port actually hails from Portugal (so it's not just a cute name). Port's association with the Brits can be traced to the Anglo nation's many conflicts with the French, which eventually led the British to look to other nations to buy wine back in the seventeenth century. To make a long story short, this search led them to Portugal. The British loved Portugal's strong, little-known red wines so much that they essentially created an industry around them—not only consuming the wines but also exporting them around the world. In fact, many of the most famous port houses of today were created back then by the entrepreneurial Brits themselves and still carry British names.

Port comes in the following diverse styles:

White Port. A rare thing, white port is of widely varying quality but when good offers notes of nuts, brown sugar, and raisins. Ferreira's White Port is one to watch for.

Ruby Port. Straightforward and fruity, ruby port is deep red (dare we say "ruby"?) in color and offers notes of dark fruits and some peppery spice. Graham's Ruby Port Six Grapes is a good one.

Tawny Port. Made light brown in color either by extended oak aging or by simply mixing white and red port, tawny port is delicious stuff. Soft and nutty compared with ruby versions, tawnies offer up caramel and licorice notes and are dynamite with nutty desserts. Warre's makes some great examples.

Vintage Port. The Rolls-Royce of any port producer's fleet, vintage port is capable of improving for one hundred years in a cellar and, like vintage Champagne, is produced only in the very best years. Once bottled, the best ones should be left alone for at least ten years, after which they offer amazingly concentrated fruit flavors backed by spice, leather, herbs, and all sorts of other good stuff. Because they develop a heavy sediment in the bottle over time, vintage port definitely needs decanting (see Chapter 8 for the lowdown on how). Watch for versions from Taylor Fladgate.

Late-Bottled Vintage Port (LBV). LBVs are similar to vintage ports, but are lighter in style and ready to drink as soon as they're released, usually about five years after they're made. Many of them have been filtered and don't require decanting, although some still do. Ramos-Pinto is a name to watch.

Single-Quinta Port. The single-quinta style, which is single-vineyard vintage port, is growing in popularity due to the increased enthusiasm for vineyard-designated wines in all styles. It's usually ready to drink sooner than vintage port, due to the additional oak it sees during maturation. Fonseca makes a good one.

Sherry: The Well-Kept Secret

Sherry, like German Riesling, is a fabulous wine with an unjustly terrible reputation. We can thank unscrupulous producers from around the world who lately "borrowed" the name of Spain's most famous fortified wine to use with sad, overly sweetened versions that bear little resemblance to this fantastic drink. To say that some of the worst sherry impersonations border on "cough syrup bad" is not an exaggeration! Happily, renewed interest in the real stuff and a decrease in the production of cheap bastardized versions are putting sherry back on the wine map, in a much better light. Let's take a closer look at what exactly sherry is, then.

Fortified, like port, with neutral grape spirit, sherry differs from Portugal's famous fortified wine in that the spirit is added to sherry after the alcoholic fermentation has finished. This brings up the key difference between sherry and all other fortified wines we've discussed: Good sherry is usually dry. I know it sounds a little odd given that this section is about sweet wines, but sherry, as a fortified wine, is almost always discussed next to its other fortified cousins, port and Madeira. So, now that we've got the dry thing out of the way, let's talk about styles of sherry.

It's in the Flor

Sherry can be produced only in a special area in the southern part of Spain near the town of Jerez, where a natural yeast called "flor" lives. Flor forms on the surface of some sherries while they're in casks, protecting them from the reductive effects of oxygen. These are smooth, relatively light wines (about 15.5 percent alcohol) called fino sherries. Flor *doesn't form* on the surface of stronger sherries that have been fortified to around 18 percent alcohol, however, because flor—like other yeasts—can't live at higher alcohol levels. In these instances, the exposure to oxygen that occurs in the absence of flor is actually a good thing, as it contributes a nutty complexity to these more powerful wines that are happily protected from complete oxidation by their higher alcoholic strength.

Let's take a closer look at the various styles of sherry.

Fino. The lightest style of sherry, finos are light brown in color and crisp in style, and they make a perfect dry aperitif. Drink chilled.

Manzanilla. Specialty sherries from the coastal town of Sanlúcar de Barrameda, Manzanillas are light in body and show an essence of saltiness. Drink these chilled.

Amontillado. Now, the nutty sherries! Deep brown in color, amontillados are aged finos that boast beautifully layered aromas, especially of nuts. Drink these slightly cooler than room temperature.

Oloroso. Even deeper brown in color than amontillados, oloroso sherries are concentrated, extremely nutty, and rich. Outstanding with good quality nuts and cheeses. Room temperature's the way to go with oloroso.

Palo Cortado. A very rare sherry, palo cortado falls between amontillado and oloroso in terms of style. Also best enjoyed at room temperature, palo cortado is praised for its pretty combination of layered aromatics and elegant body.

Caveat to the Dry Rule

Sherry being a wine, and wine being a generally complicated subject, you know that there has to be a caveat. A few good sweetened sherries *do* exist in the world, and they come in the styles described above with the addition of a sweetening agent. But don't lose sleep over this one; *most* good quality sherry is still dry!

Madeira: The Baked Wine

In a chapter in which I get to talk about sweet wines that have been rotted, frozen, and dried, it's a real pleasure to now be able to tell you about one that's been, literally, baked! Madeira is a wine that hails from a small Portuguese island by the same name, from which ships in the seventeenth century setting sail for faraway places like India would often take casks of the local wine. These wines were boosted (a.k.a. fortified) by the addition of alcohol prior to the journey in order to stand a better chance of surviving the long hot voyage in the baking hull of the ships. It didn't take long before it was discovered that the wine from Madeira tasted better—incomprehensibly—after being tossed about and, essentially, baked, in the bottoms of the boats during the long journeys. And so, as with Champagne, an industry was born as the result of an accident.

Madeira is now mostly aged in rooms or tanks called *estufas* that simulate this baking hot journey. It's known as one of the most concentrated sweet wines, boasting big flavors of nuts, spices, dried fruits like prunes and figs, molasses, coffee, and citrus essence. Depending on the style of Madeira, it can be enjoyed with salty nuts and cheeses, some Indian curries (the lighter styles) and a host of concentrated bread- and pudding-based desserts.

Here's what to look for:

Sercial. The lightest style of Madeira, sercial can actually be searingly acidic without at least ten years of aging. Fortunately, it mellows over time into lightly sweet and elegant Madeira that's ideally matched up with nuts and cheeses.

Verdelho. This Madeira is moderately sweet and a step up in body from Sercial.

Bual. This is when the big guns come out! Bual Madeira is brown in color and richly sweet on the palate. The baked wine's signature smoky character comes through on the finish.

Malmsey. Like caramel-flavored coffee, malmsey is succulently sweet and richly complex. Its deep brown color even looks like coffee, although the wine shows other notes, including baked fruits and smoke.

Other Sweeties Worth Knowing

Vins Doux Naturels (VDNs)

These dynamite sweeties are made the same way as port, but in France's southerly Languedoc-Roussillon region. There the syrupy sweet wines are made from a number of different grape varieties and in varying styles, although the most famous are the Muscat-based wines from the Beaumes-de-Venise and St.-Jean-de-Minervois regions, as well as the Grenache-focused versions from Banyuls and Rasteau. These all boast gorgeously layered aromas alongside a richly sweet full body, and are ready to drink right away after they're released. Try one instead of your usual go-to dessert wine some time; those from Banyuls, in particular, are fabulous with chocolate.

Other Ways to Say "Sweet"

In order of increasing sweetness when multiple listings appear per country:

Amabile, dolce (Italy)
Semi-seco, dulce (Spain)
Lieblich, süss (Germany)
Doux, *moelleux, liquoreux* (France)

Australian Liqueur Muscat and Liqueur Tokay

Leave it to the Aussies to make a dessert wine so incredibly sweet and powerful as to be known as the world's most powerful dessert wine. The Liqueur Muscats and Liqueur Tokays hailing from Oz are, in a word, huge. From golden honey to deep brown in hue, they're made in a megahot part of the country, in the state of Victoria, where they're partially dried (like dried wines!) before being fortified by spirit midfermentation. After this they go through still more coddling, in the form of wood aging. When they're finally released from all this activity, Liqueur Muscats and Liqueur Tokays are ready to drink right away and will stand up to any sweet food you can muster, although they're particularly divine with the richest, most concentrated chocolate desserts.

Bon Appétit

And speaking of desserts, a book on wine wouldn't be complete without guidelines on the all-important subject of wine and food pairing! The next chapter is chock-full of useful tips on matching the wines you've learned about with everything from cheeses to salads to meats to, yes, desserts. So grab yourself a snack and settle in, because you may just get hungry while reading about all this great grub.

Out with Tradition, in with Tots

Lightning struck late one night when my sister and I were brainstorming tasting ideas for my monthly HIP TASTES Events wine tastings in San Francisco. Perhaps inspired by the wonderfully simple fish and chips we were enjoying at the time, we hatched a plan for an Old School wine tasting, where we'd pair treats we'd enjoyed as kids—like mac 'n' cheese, PB&J sandwiches, gooey chocolate cake, and yes, Tater Tots—with delicious wines.

The offbeat combination of wine and so-called kiddie foods was an instant hit, getting such a slew of press in local blogs and the like before it even happened that we had to turn a handful of late-arriving guests away at the door. I have never before, or since, seen people get so excited about wine and food pairing as they did at my Old School tasting. I think there may have even been a mild skirmish over the last few Tots at the end of the evening!

What I learned that night—besides the fact that kiddie foods never get old, even though we've put on a few years—is that wine and food pairings need not be serious to be supremely enjoyable. That, and to arrive armed with more tots next time!

Chapter 6

Bon Appétit
Wine and Food

Traditionally governed by a few "classic" combinations—Cabernet Sauvignon with lamb and port with Stilton cheese come to mind—wine and food pairing lately has been shaken up by the growing popularity of experimental cuisine (think fusion) and a simultaneous desire among consumers for fresh pairings as innovative as the new foods they're sampling.

At the same time, Americans are drinking more wine than ever before, and more often. And because we generally don't eat so-called haute cuisine five nights a week, but instead enjoy everyday foods like pizza, mac 'n' cheese, and takeout, there's a very refreshing swelling of enthusiasm for wines that work well with these foods. In this chapter I'll highlight classic wine and food combos as well as some of my favorite contemporary pairings. I'll also explain how things like texture, sweetness, and alcohol content affect wine and food pairing, and leave you with a framework to come up with adventurous combinations of your own.

Because, after all, being a hip taster is all about charting your own course.

Hip to Know:
Wine and Food Pairing
Quick Reference

Without belaboring the technical facts too much, I think it's important to kick off any lesson in wine and food pairing with some fundamental guidelines that'll help you avoid mistakes and make the most of the experience. Here are a few key rules that'll help you make sound decisions every time you pair wine with food:

- Wines with high acidity (crisp whites and light reds) are the best all-around food wines.
- High-acid foods (for example, a salad with a citrusy vinaigrette) call for high-acid wines.
- High-tannin wines (big reds) are among the toughest to pair with food.
- Sweet foods always call for sweet wines.
- Heavy foods generally need similarly heavy, full-bodied wines.
- Heavy dishes *also* high in fat can work terrifically with light, sweet wines.

Route 101: Wine and Food Pairing

Imagine that you're traveling on a food and wine journey from Point A (we'll call it "hunger") to Point B (your destination, "satisfaction"). Your goal is to take the best available route—the scenic route, if you will—so that you'll enjoy your travels as much as possible. At Point A you have five roads from which to choose, all of which lead to Point B: They are texture, intensity of flavor, sweetness, acidity, and weight. Based on what you plan to eat, one of these roads and its associated wine pairings harbors the smoothest and most rewarding ride for your journey. This is because the food you've got in mind in all likelihood harbors a single dominant characteristic that aligns with one of these five choices. For a sinewy steak, that's the texture route; for a concentrated butternut squash soup, it's the intensity-of-flavor option; for a sweet-and-sour Chinese dish, that'll be the sweetness choice; for a tangy and citrusy ceviche concoction, the acidity road makes the most sense; and for a heavy ossobuco dish, you probably ought to opt for the weight route.

Getting from A to B: A Closer Look

Once you've chosen your route—that is, identified the dominant characteristic in your food—your wine selection will be much easier. This is because you have dramatically narrowed down the field of wines that will work well with your grub. But before we get into too much detail on just which wines those might be, let's take a closer look at the options to make sure you've taken the right road.

Texture Truths

Texture is an often forgotten food characteristic that plays a critical role in wine and food pairing. To that end, it's usually thought of only when its presence in food has the potential to overpower the wine. It's in these instances—

the potentially overpowering instances—that it ought to be your route of choice for your wine and food journey! Foods with textures that tend to overpower wines are those that are either excessively chewy (e.g., steak, game) or intensely mouth coating (e.g., cheese, chocolate). I'll go into more detail on how to deal with tricky foods like chocolate and cheese a little later on, in the "Wine and Food SOS" section.

Tannin. The substance found in red wine that shows up as the chalklike stuff on your teeth when you drink a really "big" red wine, tannin is one of the biggest enemies of food when it comes to wine pairing, as it makes most things taste bland and dry. Fortunately, the right foods— namely, chewy things like steak—actually serve to down-play our perception of tannin and make the wine taste more fruity and smooth. Now that's teamwork!

Three's a Crowd: Salt and Pepper and Red Wine

Salt tends to make the tannin in red wine taste more bitter than it already is, and should be avoided in excessive amounts when enjoying a good red. Pepper, on the other hand, can bring out flavors in otherwise ordinary, simple reds, making them taste more complex. The moral? Choose your season-ing wisely when drinking red.

Flavor Force

Take note: Flavor is not the same thing as weight when it comes to food! As you might imagine, there are plenty of heavy but rather neutrally flavored foods out there (doughy polenta comes to mind). Instead, when I talk about intensity of flavor I'm speaking purely about the nature of the flavors in a dish—namely, those that are very strong and therefore step into the dominant position (or obvious route) when it comes to taking a great wine and food journey. Along these lines, a classic example of highly flavorful yet decidedly *not heavy* cuisine is Thai.

With its fresh ingredients, many of which are vegetables, and piquant spices, Thai food is assertively flavored and calls for an equally assertive but light-bodied wine. Young unoaked white wines with sturdy acidity levels—Sauvignon Blanc and Riesling come to mind—make great options, since their refreshing acidity makes a great foil for the spices in the food, much in the same way a lime wedge lends levity to a hot dish. To see what I'm talking about, try a crisp white alongside a low-acid oaked white with some superspicy Thai food. You'll discover that the high-acid white stands up to the spicy flavors in the food, while the oaky wine tastes flat and unappetizing.

Low-Tannin Reds to the Rescue

Although a tannic red is a welcome partner to a meaty steak, few other foods have the stuffing to stand up to high levels of tannin in wine. That's why the best red wines for food are generally those with low to moderate levels of tannin. Not only do these more mellow reds allow you to actually taste what's on your plate, they play hospitable go-between at dinner parties, deftly working with both lighter fare (think chicken, pasta, and white meats) and the hearty foods we usually associate with red wine pairings. The best low- and moderate-tannin reds are both Old and New World Pinot Noir (fabulously popular and therefore widely available nowadays), Gamay from Beaujolais (seriously!), Italian Barbera and Dolcetto, and Cabernet Franc from France's Loire Valley. Keep your eyes peeled for these when looking for the best wines for food in the red department.

Sweet Thing

Sweetness in food needs to be matched by sweetness in wine, period. Of all the possible routes for your journey outlined in this section, sweetness is the least flexible (meaning, if you've got a sweet dish, you'd better be taking the sweet road!). This is because supersweet things such as ice cream make all but the sweetest wines taste thin and tart by comparison. As an example, if you've ever tried to continue drinking a dry table wine after dinner with your dessert, you've probably noted that the dry wine tastes un-appetizingly acidic, even metallic, and definitely out of place. If you haven't tried this, don't—you'll regret it! Instead, just remember that sweet needs sweet, and reach for a correspondingly sweet wine.

Caveat on When Sweet and Savory Come Together

There has to be a gray area or wine and food pairing wouldn't be so much fun! Something that can be puzzling at first but ultimately resolvable is what to do when a mid-meal (read: savory) dish includes significant sweet overtones. If you're wondering what incarnation this sort of thing might take, think of your Thanksgiving turkey with its sweet cranberry garnish. On the one hand, turkey is a dry, savory, and most certainly *not* sweet food. When you add cranberry sauce to the mix, however, it takes on a whole new identity. This sweetness becomes a focus of the dish, and your wine selection ought to reflect that.

In these middle-of-the-road situations it's best to reach for a semisweet wine. I come back to German Riesling because it's such a fabulous wine for food (thanks to its sturdy acidity level) and often has a touch of sweetness. Those labeled Kabinett are great bets, because they're only mildly sweet—just the perfect amount for your mildly sweet dish. Other good options include Alsatian and some New World Gewürztraminers, many of which marry a dash of sweetness with a rich body that's perfect for hearty turkey.

Acidity Answered

My favorite thing to talk about when explaining why it's so critical that acidity in food be matched by acidity in wine is the megafresh fish dish traditionally from South America that we call ceviche (suh-vee-chay). The dish, which shows up frequently in California cuisine due to its light, healthy nature, is, quite simply, fish "cooked" exclusively in citrus juices. This works because the concentrated acidity we find in citrus fruits like lemons and limes kills harmful bacteria that might be hanging around in the fish. What's left is the fish in its freshest state; it is usually served with a sprinkling of veggies or tropical fruits and a side of chips.

Foods that are rife with acidity, such as lemon- and lime-doused ceviche, must be matched up with wines of similar acidic strength, or the wine will taste hopelessly flat and thin (a.k.a. flabby) by comparison. This is because wine's own natural acidity can be overshadowed by that in high-acid foods, and the result is a combination that's un-appetizingly out of balance. I usually opt for megacrisp Sauvignon Blanc from New Zealand or Chile on occa-sions when I'll be tucking into high-acid foods like cevi-che, although assertive Austrian Grüner Veltliner and refreshing Vinho Verde from Portugal will also do the trick.

Acid Reflex

As with anything else in life, too much acid is never a good thing. We add acid regularly to our foods—most commonly in the form of tangy vinaigrette dressings on salads—and if you're not careful, you can find yourself so far into acidity no-man's-land that there's simply *no* wine that can save you (read: stand up to all this sourness!). Acid, although all right in moderate amounts, is a sworn enemy of wine in excessive quantities. The moral: Try not to douse your salad with too much of that super-tangy vinaigrette! Or don't plan on enjoying your wine if you do.

A Weighty Issue

Last but most definitely not least, the issue of weight in a dish should also be taken into account when pairing wine with food. Weight in food comes from a couple of places—the nature of the food itself (e.g., vegetables, pastas, and meats all have varying weights) as well as the way in which it's cooked. Rare red meats, for example, are indisputably heavy foods, calling for a weighty red wine to stand up to their power and structure. But certain pastas can also be elevated into the realm of so-called heavy foods if they're prepared accordingly. For example, anyone who's had a megarich fettuccine alfredo, with its hearty cream and butter sauce, will agree that this Italian specialty is most definitely a heavy dish.

Along these lines, anything that's been prepared in a heavy sauce, reduced, or smoked will in all likelihood come out the other side as a heavy dish. Those that have been steamed, boiled, poached, or not cooked at all, on the other hand, will usually turn out on the lighter side. Wines with elevated alcohol and tannin levels are those we consider heavy, and as such should be matched up to hearty fare, while those with lower alcohol and more subdued tannin settle comfortably into the light category. And when it comes to a megalight dish like a cheese soufflé, you'll want to pair that light-as-air treat with a similarly light wine with creamy notes, such as a crisp white Chablis (French Chardonnay).

Caveat to the Weight Debate

Occasionally, certain heavy foods call for light wines to lend them a little levity (or, seen another way, some foods are so heavy that pairing them with correspondingly heavy wines is like adding butter to cream—it's just too much). These include dishes that are extremely high in fat, like the French delicacy foie gras. Made from the fattened-up livers of geese and ducks, foie gras is one of the fattiest foods around, and it's sometimes best offset by the likes of a light German Riesling with a hint of sweetness.

Let's Get Sauced

As hinted at previously in the weight section, a sauce can dramatically change a dish's makeup. On certain rare occasions when the sauce is strong enough, it trumps all other considerations for wine and food pairing, and should be your main guide in deciding which wine to pair with your food. Reduction sauces and glazes, such as those often used in steak houses, call for a full-bodied fruity red, such as an Australian Shiraz or a California Cabernet Sauvignon. Heavy white sauces based on cream and butter should be matched by a medium- to full-bodied white wine like Chardonnay—white Burgundy and New World renderings from California's Sonoma come to mind—while wine-based white sauces call for a white wine with strong acidity, such as Chablis, Sauvignon Blanc, or Chenin Blanc. In the case of highly piquant béarnaise and horseradish-based sauces, you're best off reaching for our favorite tricky food wine, German Riesling.

Bon Voyage!

Once you've selected the route for your wine and food journey you'll be on your way to better pairings and, hopefully, an enjoyable ride. Just don't forget to take the occasional side road along the way—some of the best pairings are discovered when you veer from the "correct" path!

Putting Wine and Food Pairing to Work

Now that you're familiar with the key food and wine pairing guidelines, let's talk about matching up the stuff in the context of the real world—today's eclectic global dining environment.

Starters

The beginning of any meal almost invariably involves foods containing lots of salt (think nuts, cheese, chips, and pastry-based starters like miniquiches). Because salt amplifies our perception of tannin in wine, your best bets here are crisp whites and low-tannin reds. The brisk acidity in good starter wines plays the same role as salt—both serve to make your mouth water, something that puts you in the perfect state to enjoy the rest of your meal.

Starter Wines. When getting started, reach for a Loire Valley Sauvignon Blanc or a superlight and crisply acidic Muscadet from the same region, an Alsatian Riesling, a *trocken* ("dry") Riesling from Germany, a refreshing Italian white like Vermentino or Verdicchio, or a Spanish Albariño. Low-tannin reds, including food-friendly Pinot Noir, Barbera, Cabernet Franc, and Gamay are also good bets if going red is a must.

Quick Note on Substance and Body. Save the big guns—full-bodied or complex wines—for later in the meal, opting instead for more simple, straightforward wines with your starters. Just as you wouldn't devour a rich ossobuco concoction before a delicate seafood risotto, you're best off starting things with the lightest wines and working your way up through the weight spectrum as your meal progresses. Besides, as with a good plot line in a movie, you want to build up to the climax rather than start with it!

Salads

Inherently difficult with wine, salads present a unique challenge to diners. Greens—and pretty much all vegetables, for that matter—tend to make wines taste metallic, especially reds.* In nine meals out of ten I'd stick to white wine when it comes to anything of the vegetable persuasion. Among whites, the best wines for salads and veggies are those with crisp acidity and—ideally—a hint of green-

---

* See "Wine and Food SOS" a little later on for more on how to cope with tricky veggies, like asparagus and artichokes.

ness to them. If the salad has nuts, like pine nuts or pecans, feel free to step up your wine selection to a white with a little more body, like Pinot Gris.

Salad Wines. Portuguese Vinho Verde ("green wine") is a great and easy-to-remember choice for salads, as is Austrian Grüner Veltliner, which has a peppery flavor that works terrifically with the bitterness found in greens. Sauvignon Blanc—especially from New Zealand—is a nobrainer here as well, with its grassy and vegetal notes (in fact, it's often described as tasting of asparagus and green peas!).

Fish

There are many fish in the sea, as the popular saying goes, and as you might imagine, there's a correspondingly numerous collection of fish dishes to go along with all of these swimmers. This has as much to do with what kind of fish you've got on your plate (e.g., shellfish versus sea bass) as with how it's prepared: Even the most neutral fish dishes can be radically altered by the addition of a rich butter reduction sauce, a piquant chile lime glaze, or whatever other sauce du jour a chef can cook up. Frying, another popular avenue for fish preparation, also calls for unique pairings. No matter what, if your fish is packing some serious influence thanks to its cooking method or sauce, you'll need to consider that as well as the kind of fish when pairing it with wine.

Fish Wines. Fried fish, with its richness and oily texture, calls for a white wine with some sweetness (to counteract the richness) and high acidity (to cut through the fat); my favorites are German Rieslings of the Kabinett level as well as off-dry sparkling wines. Demi-sec Vouvray (Chenin Blanc) from the Loire Valley in France is another great choice, since Chenin packs some serious acid alongside its sweetness.

Simply prepared shellfish and most varieties of white fish work well with light- to medium-bodied whites of a not too assertive nature, so skip the New Zealand Sauvignon Blanc and reach instead for its more mellow French counterparts, Sancerre and Pouilly-Fumé. Crisp Chardonnays (generally speaking, those from the Old World and cooler New World locales) work here as well. For the richest fish, like lobster and scallops, feel free to step it up to full-bodied whites like New World Chardonnay, Viognier, and anything from Alsace.

Pasta

Like many a fish dish, pasta concoctions run the gamut of styles, weights, and flavors. This is because pasta, a somewhat neutral substance on its own, takes on the inherent nature of whatever sauce is put on it and runs with it. Simple pasta dishes prepared with little more than olive oil and a dash of freshly shaved parmesan are the most neutrally flavored, while heartier renderings made with rich meats and stewlike sauces tip the scales in the other direction.

Pasta Wines. Let the sauce be your guide in selecting a wine for your pasta. Olive oil–based pastas are the most flexible; the key with these is to make sure you don't overpower the dish. Stick to light- to medium-bodied whites and light reds. If your pasta's made with a white sauce—which usually involves cream or butter—reach for a suitably full-bodied white, like Chardonnay, Marsanne, or Pinot Gris from France or Oregon. Pastas made with tomato-based sauces call for medium-bodied, fruity reds like Dolcetto, Barbera, or Chianti. Those with meat-based sauces, on the other hand, need something stronger: In these cases reach for robust, earthy reds without too much tannin, such as Brunello di Montalcino, Châteauneuf-du-Pape from France's Rhône Valley, or Sicilian reds made from the newly hip Nero d'Avola grape.

Beef and Game

Finally, the "big stuff"! These hearty dishes are the climax of the evening and what you've been building up to over your earlier courses. It makes sense, then, to serve a suitably climactic wine. But it bears noting that not all meats are made the same: Although everything in this category is rather rich, some—such as lighter meats, quail, and chicken—are a significant step down in strength from their most meaty peers, which include big game like boar, moose, elk, and venison. And, as with everything else that graces the table, you need to take the dish's cooking method into account here as well.

Generally, roasted meats are the most succulent and wine-friendly of the beef and game bunch. Slow cooking allows these meats to show their rich and savory flavors to best advantage while maintaining a delicacy of flavor ideally suited to wine. These meats work beautifully with classy reds with some age to them, as the delicate flavors of the meat won't mask the complexity these beauties have developed over time.

Beef and Game Wines. Roast lamb is a classic match to old Bordeaux (for a hip substitute try an older Napa Cab or Italian Super-Tuscan), and roast quail is a gorgeous pairing with a top Pinot Noir, such as aged red Burgundy. Merlot works beautifully with a delicate filet mignon. And anything grilled or of a seriously concentrated nature (think about the big game items here) calls for a younger, more concentrated red. This is the time to pull out the big guns—Aussie Shiraz, young Bordeaux reds, Argentinian Malbec, Chilean Carmenère, California Zinfandel, hearty reds from the south of France . . . you get the idea. The bigger the better!

Dessert

As you know after reading Chapter 5, there are lots of sweet wines out there to choose from. For the most concentrated sweet desserts, such as flourless chocolate cake and ice cream, you'll want to reach for the most powerful dessert wines, including but certainly not limited to port and Muscats from Australia and France. Desserts of moderate sweetness and intensity, such as crème brûlée, call for a similarly medium-bodied sticky; Sauternes and ice wine work great here. The lightest sweet things, which include pastry- and fruit-based desserts, partner terrifically with the lightest sweet wines; my favorite, Moscato d'Asti, is a dynamite choice, although sweet German Riesling (especially Spätlese) also works swimmingly.

Hip Matches Made in Heaven

You didn't think I'd leave you hanging without talking about wines to pair with the foods we eat most often, did you?! In the proverbial world of wine and food pairing, that would be like me sending you off on your journey without a road map. And that would be *so* not hip. So get ready—now's the time to learn the really important stuff: What to drink with the stuff we eat every day.

Pizza

With its sweet-tasting tomato sauce, pizza calls for a red wine with similarly sweet flavors and relatively low tannin. California Zinfandel is my favorite wine for pizza, since it has a peppery quality that perfectly echoes the black pepper in tomato sauce. Côtes-du-Rhône reds from the south of France are also good bets for pizza, as are their peers from the nearby Languedoc-Roussillon, a great area for robust value reds. Besides these, most New World reds without excessive tannin will do the trick for pizza, since they've got the fruity sweetness pizza needs.

Mexican

Growing up in California, I've been privy to some fantastic Mexican food over the years. With its emphasis on

meat and fried corn-based goodies, Mexican fare is hearty stuff that can pack some serious heat (think of all those jalapeño chiles!). Add to these factors the abundant salt on the chips that usually accompany Mexican food and you've got a pretty complex combo of flavors. For Mexican dishes that aren't excessively spicy and don't contain red meat, opt for medium-bodied whites with ripe fruit and sturdy acidity; the best I've found so far are Australian Rieslings, most of which are technically dry but have ripe fruit flavors that work well with the richness found in Mexican fare.

For dishes with dark meat and a low heat quotient reach for ripe, round medium-bodied reds; most Spanish reds work swimmingly here, particularly the round, fruity versions coming out of newly cool regions Bierzo and Yecla. When there's spice involved, go for *trocken* (dry) German Riesling or Cabernet Franc from France's Loire Valley. Dry sparklers are also good options.

BBQ

Because grilling involves cooking something quickly over dry heat, the process intensifies flavors in whatever's being grilled while imparting a distinctive flavor of, well, smoke. This means that grilled meats can stand up to full-bodied, oaky wines, since the toasted notes of the oak complement those of the smoked meat. And because grilling also usually involves a marinade or sauce of a sweet nature, it makes sense that *fruity* full-bodied wines work best.

So, pull out the big guys here, the souped-up oaked reds from California (Zin or Petite Sirah and BBQ are fabulous together), South America (Malbec works well with grilled dark meats), South Africa (if ever there's a time to serve Pinotage, it's with BBQ), and Australia. This is certainly not an exhaustive list, but you get the point. If your grilled food is of a lighter persuasion, reach for an oaky white, like Chardonnay. For an off-the-beaten-path hip alternative for grilled meats of all kinds, seek out an Australian sparkling Shiraz.

Sandwiches and Wraps

Sandwiches, with their bread carbs, are rather hearty items, and call for wines with at least moderate body. Besides this, they run the gamut when it comes to flavor combinations, thanks to the innumerable ingredients with which they can be made. With 'wiches, then, you're best off sticking to the wine and food pairing guidelines outlined at the outset of this chapter, selecting wines based on the dominant quality (e.g., intensity of flavor, weight, texture, acidity, or sweetness) in the sandwich at hand. Besides these qualities, let the casual nature of the 'wich help you choose your wine.

My favorite wine for heartier sandwiches like those containing cured or grilled meats is a Beaujolais-Villages red, a fruity, young wine that's perfect for quaffing at lunch. And for most any sandwich I like sparkling wines, especially traditional method versions, as their yeasty flavors mimic those of bread, while their sturdy acidity stands up to all kinds of different fillings, from grilled vegetables and cheese on up to meat.

Sushi

Nothing perplexes diners looking for wine pairings more than raw fish (for good reason). Add spicy wasabi and tangy-sweet ginger to the raw fish and you've got a seriously perplexing combination of flavors! Hearkening back to the wine and food pairing guidelines outlined earlier, we take our cue in the case of sushi from the strongest element in this mix—the spicy wasabi—in choosing our wine. Because sweetness is the absolute best foil to spiciness of all kinds, the best wines for sushi are off-dry (read: slightly sweet) whites, whose negligible tannin doesn't overpower this delicacy. Sake—Japanese rice wine—is the best option for sushi, although Kabinett and some Spätlese-level German Rieslings are also great options.

Burgers and Fries

Nowadays, it seems like you can get everything fast: Movies are available on demand, e-mail has made correspondence lightning fast, and online shopping makes buying things as quick as a single click. Fast food—whether in the form of a gratifyingly greasy burger and fries or a more healthy sub sandwich—epitomizes this quick lifestyle and isn't going away anytime soon, in spite of efforts by many an anti-obesity lobbying group. Personally, I love nothing more than the occasional well-deserved burger binge, and, being the wine nut that I am, you can probably imagine I've tracked down at least a few wines worth knocking back with burgers.

Sparkling wines with high levels of acidity are ideal with fatty foods like burgers and fries, as they're able to cut through the fat and provide a pretty good palate cleanser in the form of their crisply satisfying bubbles. But don't waste Champagne on fast food; instead reach for Spain's refreshingly inexpensive Champagne look-alike, Cava. Simple German Rieslings with a hint of sweetness are also great choices, as their sweetness counteracts the intense saltiness of most fast foods. And, if a red's in order, go for simple, medium-bodied New World numbers with low tannin, like lighter Zins.

Picnics, Etc.

I love picnics because they afford the rare opportunity to eat outdoors, something that I find transforms even the most regular meals into something altogether more momentous. The key thing to remember when choosing wines for picnics is that they ought to be of light to medium body and simple in character. A picnic isn't the time to bring out wines to dissect and discuss—it's a time to enjoy your company, the sunshine, and the occasion.

There's no better white wine for picnics than Italy's wonderfully floral and straightforward Prosecco, and I also like fresh and easy-to-enjoy Crémant sparkling wines from France for outdoor meals. Along these lines, any other light, refreshing white will work (think Muscadet, Sauvignon Blanc, Pinot Grigio). Reach for reds from France's Beaujolais, fruity New World Pinot Noir (I especially like the light-bodied versions coming out of New Zealand for picnics), and light Italian reds, like Dolcetto d'Alba.

Bonus Round: Wine with Cheese

A lesson on wine and food pairing wouldn't be complete without a section on the all-important subject of wine and cheese pairing!

Cheese: Wine's Undercover Enemy

But first, I have to reveal a couple of shocking facts. The first: Cheese, with its gluey, mouth-coating texture, is really a natural enemy of wine. Why? Because the high fat content in cheese leaves a gooey film in our mouths that makes it difficult for us to taste wine. Also, the saltiness in cheese exacerbates our perception of tannin, making big red wines taste absurdly dry, clumsy, and unappetizing. This is because salt amplifies the tannin in wine, much as it amplifies the flavors in food (which in the case of food is usually a good thing).

Fortunately, certain wines come armed with special powers that help them overcome these problems. These low-tannin (mostly white) wines are the cheese-friendly wines of the world, and with their assistance we can all get over the goo and taste both the cheese and the wine in all their glory. Besides white wines, low-tannin reds like Pinot Noir, Barbera, and Gamay work adequately with cheese, too. The most difficult wines to match up to cheeses are big-bodied tannic reds (think Cab, Nebbiolo, Syrah). For this reason, your best cheese bets for red wines are hard cheeses, whose grainy texture somewhat mimics that of tannin.

Back to Fifth Grade: Compare and Contrast

Remember when you learned in fifth grade that time-honored literary form that's known as the "compare and contrast essay"? Right up there in educational importance with the mighty "five-paragraph essay," the compare and contrast format was simple but powerful when it came to explaining complex subjects (or so you thought at the time).

Wine and cheese pairing is a lot like that essay. There are two obvious and usually rewarding routes you can travel when it comes to matching wine with cheese: You can either compare the flavors of the two or, you guessed it, contrast them. Certain cheeses just happen to partner well with wines of similar taste profiles (these are destined for the comparison track) while others fare better when their tricky qualities—chief among them excessive saltiness—are offset by something in the wine, usually sweetness (these, obviously, fall into the contrasting camp).

Cheese 411

Popular Comparative Wine and Cheese Pairings

Goat cheese (a.k.a. chèvre) and Sauvignon Blanc
Why: Because goat cheese is high in acidity, as is Sauvignon Blanc.

Cheddar and full-bodied, rich New World Chardonnay
Why: Because they're both buttery and nutty at the same time, yum!

Parmigiano-Reggiano and Chianti Riserva
Why: Because the grainy texture in Parmesan echoes the tannin in this red wine.

Swiss Gruyère and Alsatian Pinot Gris
Why: Because the nutty and fruity notes in Gruyère are perfectly answered in this white that often boasts low notes of nuts.

Popular Contrasting Wine and Cheese Pairings

Blue cheese and sweet wines, especially port (with Stilton) and Sauternes (with Roquefort)
Why: Because blue cheese is supersalty, and salty and sweet combos rock.

Creamy Cheeses (e.g., Brie) and Old World Pinot Noir
Why: The rich, runny texture and nutty flavor of these cheeses is offset by Pinot's refreshing acidity and warm fruit flavors.

Swiss Raclette and French Beaujolais
Why: The earthy and beefy flavors of this cow's milk cheese that's meant for melting are ideally offset by the fresh fruitiness of light red Beaujolais.

Entertaining with Cheese

For tips on putting together a killer cheese board at home, check out Chapter 8, "Wine at Home."

And the Winner Is . . . Sweet Wine!

Prepare yourself for the final stunner of my wine and cheese pairing exposé: The all-around best wines for cheese, hands down, are sweet wines. Extremely low in tannin, sweet wines don't do battle with the goo, and their sweetness is the best possible foil to cheese's characteristic saltiness. So, next time you're pairing wine with cheese, reach for one of the following recommended pairings, or pretty much any sweet wine: ice wine, Sauternes, Auslese-level Riesling from Germany, or tawny port.

It's in the Cheese

Here's an overview of the kinds of cheeses you can expect to find at a good artisanal cheese shop (something definitely worth seeking out if you plan to do much cheese tasting), although growing numbers of nicer grocery stores have begun carrying lots of these yummy items, too.

Creamy Cheese. Epitomized by the all-popular Brie, creamy cheeses take their name (and their runny texture) from their superhigh fat content. They're among the most difficult to pair with wine—second only to supersalty blue

cheeses—due to their intensely mouth-coating texture. Besides Brie, well-known creamy cheeses include Camembert and Époisses, superstinky numbers from France that are so creamy you sometimes need a spoon to spread them. Match these up with low- to medium-tannin reds such as Pinot Noir, Cru Beaujolais, and Dolcetto. They also work well with whites with sturdy acidity and a hint of creaminess; I like French Chablis (Chardonnay) as well as Chardonnay from cool Western Australia.

Goat Cheese. Often referred to by its French name, chèvre, goat cheese is a step up in firmness from creamy cheese. It's usually quite aromatic and boasts a tangy acidity that's unique to cheeses made from goat's milk. The best-known versions come from France's Loire Valley, where the cheese's tangy nature is perfectly at home with the region's equally assertive Sauvignon Blancs (think Sancerre and Pouilly-Fumé). Watch for the cheese in its characteristic "log" form, or in little rounds, both of which are widely available, and pair it up with Sauvignon Blanc from the

Loire or New Zealand, crisp whites from northern Spain, or light reds from the Loire; the best are from the appellations of Chinon and Bourgueil.

Semisoft Cheese. If any category of cheese gets overlooked on a regular basis, it's this middle group, sometimes referred to as semisoft and, at other times, semihard (I know, confusing!). Made up of mostly cow's and sheep's milk cheeses, semisoft cheeses have a nutty richness to them that's fabulous with a number of wines, especially rich whites. My favorite of all semisoft cheeses is Tomme de Savoie from the foothills of the Alps in France; Switzerland's Gruyère; and Spain's Manchego are other delicious semisoft cheeses. Match them up with rich white wines like those from Alsace and medium-bodied reds with a hint of earthiness, like those from Rioja and France's Rhône Valley.

Hard Cheese. At last, a cheese category in which red wines reign supreme! The most famous hard cheese is probably Italy's illustrious Parmigiano-Reggiano, which achieves its firm structure thanks to a mandatory aging period of at least fourteen months. As mentioned earlier, the grainy texture that develops in hard cheeses over time is what makes them such good companions to the tannin in red wine. Other well-known hard cheeses include Cheddar and Italy's Asiago. No matter where they're from, hard cheeses work best when paired with most medium- to full-bodied reds, as well as with a handful of sturdy white wines. Nothing-shy-about-me New World Chardonnay is a good bet if you must pair hard cheese with a white, and sweet wines are also, as always, good bets.

Cheese 411, Part II

When in Doubt, Go for a Regional Pairing

Regional pairings are just what they sound like—wines and cheeses that go together because they grow together. These are the no-brainer combos of the wine and cheese world—and they're usually delicious. Try these:

Asiago and light Italian reds, including Dolcetto d'Alba and Barbera d'Asti
Why: This crowd-pleasing semihard cow's milk cheese from Italy's Veneto is perfect for light- to medium-bodied reds from the boot.

Manchego and Spanish reds, including Crianza Rioja and reds from Navarra
Why: Young versions of this semisoft sheep's milk cheese work beautifully with fruity reds; match up aged Manchegos with fuller-bodied Spanish reds (e.g., those from Penedès, Ribera del Duero).

Chaource and Champagne
Why: Because this soft, acidic cheese that's similar to Brie is perfectly at home with yeasty, acidic Champagne; a fabulous combo!

Blue Cheese. Some of the most famous wine and cheese pairings originate with blue cheese, but like so many things in life with "two sides," so do some of the worst. Basically, anything that's not sweet or rather high in acidity will taste vile with blue cheese, which is remarkably strong and incredibly salty (that's a double blow to all but the most sturdy wines). As a rule, sweet wines work best here, especially fortified sweet wines, including port and Madeira. Roquefort is a classic match with *Botrytis*-affected (read: nobly rotten) Sauternes, while Stilton is heavenly with vintage or tawny port. These are actually two of the most famous wine and food pairings in the world! Also try fruity, somewhat older reds, including those from Rioja (watch for *reserva* bottlings).

Wine and Food SOS:
Difficult Foods for Wine and How to Deal

We've covered cheese, one of the most difficult foods to pair with wine, but there are a few other tough items that merit mentioning.

Veggies: Artichokes and Asparagus

Both artichokes and asparagus make most wines taste metallic and bitter. Squeezing a little lemon over these veggies will mitigate some of this affront to wine, as will pairing them up with crisp white wines with a hint of greenness. New Zealand Sauvignon Blanc is hands down the best option, and Grüner Veltliner and Vinho Verde work tolerably, too.

Eggs

Eggs and wine are a tough combo, no doubt about it. With their runny, mouth-coating texture, egg yolks mask our ability to taste wine, while the texture of many other egg dishes (think of a porous, creamy quiche) is also a challenge. When it comes to matching egg dishes to wine, your best bet is to seek out something else in the dish besides the egg with which to work: For a quiche and all other cream- and cheese-based egg dishes reach for a medium- to full-bodied white wine that works well with these rich additions (think Pinot Blanc or Viognier); for eggs prepared with lemon-influenced sauces, reach for Sauvignon Blanc. Sparkling wines are always a good bet, too.

Fruit

When tucking into a fruit salad or any other dish in which fruit plays a starring role, reach for an unoaked white wine with some sweetness to it. Oak is fundamentally at odds with the freshness and sweetness found in fruit, two things that ought to be echoed in the wine you choose. Italy's light and fizzy Moscato d'Asti is a perfect choice for fruit salads, as it's not only sweet but is one of the few wines that actually smell like grapes! Kabinett and Spätlese-level German Rieslings also work well with fruit, as do *Botrytis*-affected whites like Sauternes when it comes to fruity desserts.

Chocolate

Chocolate is my favorite food *ever,* and since wine is also a favorite of mine, you might guess I've gone to pains to get to the bottom of how to best match up these two delights. Chocolate, like cheese, is extremely high in fat, and as a result it's got a gooey mouth-coating texture that deals a serious blow to all but the strongest wines. So when it comes to chocolate, reach for sweet high-alcohol wines, especially fortified sweeties like port, Madeira, and VDNs (*vins doux naturels*) from the south of France. The high alcohol in these wines cuts through fatty chocolate's goo while their sweetness matches that found in chocolate. Cheers to *that.*

The Next Level

Now that we've got the whole food-and-wine-pairing thing down, it's time to put your new smarts to practical use. The next chapter discusses how to order wine in restaurants and includes advice on avoiding embarrassing pitfalls, overspending, and winding up with a bad bottle. It'll all come in handy the next time you're in the hot seat— meaning you've just been asked to place the wine order for your whole table—or simply find yourself in a new place with a hankering to try something different.

First Date with
a Sommelier

I once had a first date with a guy who went to really impressive lengths to make sure he selected a killer bottle of wine. First, he'd phoned the restaurant beforehand, had the wine list faxed over, then put in a call to the wine director himself to walk through the options and home in on a great bottle. His selection—a *premier cru* red Burgundy from an outstanding year—was dynamite and, although the relationship wasn't meant to be, he still scored major points in my book with his dedication to the task.

Picking a wine off a restaurant list can be daunting for anyone, not just a guy with an impending date with a sommelier. This is because every restaurant has a different wine list, and picking the perfect wine from the many and sometimes confusing selections can be a lot of pressure. Happily, there *is* method to the madness of ordering and enjoying wine in restaurants. In this chapter I'll walk you through the three key steps involved in landing a great bottle in any restaurant: interpreting a restaurant's wine list, making your selection, and placing your order. I'll also provide helpful tips like how to get the help you need from a sommelier or server, how to know when you're being overcharged, and how to send a bad bottle back with tact.

Chapter 7

Wine out in the World

How Many Were My Producers

As a sommelier, I often wish I had an encyclopedic memory. Why? Because there are so many producers of the good stuff out there it can seem daunting, if not downright impossible, to recall even a fraction of them when taking in a restaurant's wine list. In California alone there are more than two thousand wineries, most of which release new wines every year, each of which differs from the previous years' wines. And globally, there are many, many more wineries, all of which release new wines with regularity, just as they do in California. Whew!

This is why any humble (and honest) sommelier will tell you that it's impossible to get to know every producer out there. Which leads to another important question: How, then, do you place a competent order in a restaurant when the experts themselves can't even recognize all of the wineries? If you just answered, "You need more information," then you're absolutely on track: Instead of relying on your knowledge of wine "brands" as you might when shopping for clothes, cars, or a watch, you'll need to consider other factors besides just the wine's producer before placing your order in a restaurant.

Step 1: Making Sense of the List

Traditionally, not long after you'd been seated at a restaurant a thick leather-bound wine list would arrive at your table. More often than not, the tome's lengthy selection would include three broad categories—sparkling, white, and red wines—usually arranged in that order, with dessert wines at the end, or possibly on a separate list. Occasionally, restaurants would shake things up by listing the wines by region—for more formal spots this was usually predominantly Italy and France, with a little United States of America thrown in for good measure.

Today, lists come in all shapes and sizes and can be arranged in many different ways. Before you get intimidated by this shaking up of wine-listing rationale, let me assure you that these changes are often for the better; in fact, some of the new categories into which wines are broken out actually make more sense than the old sparkling-white-red-dessert format, and can even make your task of choosing a wine a whole lot easier. Besides these happy reorganizations, many of today's lists include wines from all over the world, and some also carry descriptions, lending still more clarity to your decision-making process.

Lowdown on List Rationale

Most restaurant wine lists are organized by one of the following criteria:

- color (e.g., white, pink, red)
- region of origin
- grape variety
- wine weight
- suggested food pairing(s)

When to Order a Beer or a Cocktail

While it can be unsettling to open a wine list on which you don't recognize a single producer, the opposite is even more frightening. You know what I'm talking about—the lists that contain a short selection from mainstream producers, each of which you recognize as a widely available, generic brand. These are the lists that have been put together with little thought and even less consideration for the spot's patrons. When you come upon a list like this, chances are good that the food will be as unimaginative as the wine, and I recommend hightailing it outta there fast! If you can't (like if you're stuck for a coworker's birthday or similar inflexible situation), order a beer or a cocktail instead, and spare yourself the pain of drinking what's in all likelihood boring wine.

A Question of Color

The most standard and widely used strategy for organizing a wine list is by the color of the wines; these lists are intuitive but not necessarily easy to use. The reason is that, aside from grouping the wines into these easy-to-understand buckets, a color-organized list does little else to assist you in making your selection. As I mentioned earlier, it's unrealistic to expect that you'll consistently be able to order wines out in the world based on your knowledge of producers alone.

So, how to deal? First, look at where the wines are from. Even in the absence of regional subcategories, most wine lists will include a wine's region in the listing, e.g., 2001 Robert Mondavi Cabernet Sauvignon, **Napa Valley**, **California**. This is almost always the case for New World wines, although with Old World wines this process is a little tougher, due to the fact that many Old World wines take their names from ambiguous-sounding places rather than from grapes. A 1996 Château Lynch-Bages **Pauillac,** for example, hails from Bordeaux, but you would know that only if you were familiar with the Bordeaux subregion of Pauillac! This is a great example of why it's not a bad idea to familiarize yourself with some of the better subregions of Bordeaux, which I've listed in the Appendix, along with recent good vintages from the area.

Another lifeline you can grab onto when perusing a color-organized list is that of grape variety, when it's listed. Again, New World wines will be kinder to you here, since many of them contain their dominant grape variety in the name, as does the Mondavi Cab mentioned a moment ago. You may also recall that these are what we call "varietal wines" because they're named for—you guessed it—their grape varieties. Old World wines are tougher: Returning to the Bordeaux example, you would know that a Lynch-Bages red is made mostly of Cabernet Sauvignon only if you were familiar with the region of Pauillac and its wines. If you're thinking that this all sounds incredibly confusing, you're absolutely right—it's also another reason wine lists are evolving to become more user friendly.

Regional Rationale

A wine list arranged by region is a step up in terms of ease of use from its color-organized peers. This is because we can infer several things about a wine based on its region of origin, the most fundamental of which is whether it's from the Old World or the New World. Better yet, many regionally organized lists contain subcategories within regional groups separating whites from reds (and, in some cases, rosés and sparklers, too). Already, as you can see, we've got lots more information to work with than we had with our color-only list!

Another reason I like regional lists is that regional wine and food pairings—like regional wine and cheese pairings—are no-brainer combos that usually taste great because, as a famous food writer once wisely said, "What grows together goes together." So, if you're eating Italian, you're probably in good shape selecting an Italian wine. You'll have an even better experience the more precise you get with your regional match; for example, northwestern Italian wines pair best with cuisine from that area, where dishes include more cream than you'll find in dishes from the rest of the country, where the cooking is done mostly with olive oil. Wines from the northwest reflect this richer style, as they should. Ask your server for help in fine-tuning your regional wine and food match.

A Grape Match

One of most widely used styles of wine list you'll come across today, the list organized by grape variety is ideally suited to our New World–honed understanding of wine. On these lists, all of the Chardonnays will be grouped together, as will all the Pinot Noirs, the Cabernet Sauvignons, and so forth. The categories usually lump together both Old World and New World wines, giving us welcome assistance when it comes to IDing the varietally ambiguous Old World suspects that don't include grape variety in their names. Blended wines will be listed either in the categories aligning with the dominant grape in their blend (e.g., Cabernet Sauvignon for most Bordeaux and American Meritage blends) or in a separate category.

Within these lists, categories may contain other information besides just grape variety. For example, wines may be listed in order of increasing weight, price, or vintage. The price and vintage indicators will be obvious, but the weight distinction takes a bit of studying to deduce. This may be what's going on if, for example, the first Chardonnays listed are French, followed by fuller-bodied New World versions. If you come across a list like this, consider yourself lucky—these other indicators are more clues that'll help you find the ideal wine for your food!

Weight Watchers

Given that weight is an important consideration when it comes to wine and food pairing, lists arranged by the weight of wines (e.g., from crisp and light to medium-bodied to full and rich) make a lot of sense. Generally, these lists include signposts differentiating whites from reds and, if you're lucky, rosés and sparkling wines as well. The rationale behind these lists is straightforward, but it's important to note that they're only as reliable as the people who create them, since an element of subjectivity unavoidably comes into play in deciding which whites are light and crisp, which are full and rich, and so on.

Still, so long as they're well crafted, wine lists organized by weight are some of the most innovative ones out there, and can be remarkably effective in helping you choose wines that will work well with your food. But you still have to work here: Most important, you'll need to decide whether your food calls for a wine of similar or contrasting weight. Hearkening back to Chapter 6, you may recall that this depends on the dish. Most dishes are best paired with wines of similar weight, although some of the richest (read: fatty) things are best paired with lighter wines that mitigate their heaviness.

Food Matches

I have mixed feelings about lists that break out wines by the foods they're meant to partner. Besides making the obvious assumption that you have the same wine and food proclivities as whoever put the list together, these lists also run the risk of steering diners away from potentially interesting combinations, especially those of a contrasting nature. These lists tend to stick to similar combinations (e.g., acid with acid, spicy with spicy), which although often good aren't the only ways to go when it comes to wine and food pairing.

Still, I think the goal of these lists—to help diners home in on wines they'll enjoy with their meal—is a good one. In fact, for folks who don't know a ton about wine, these lists can be quite helpful. My advice to those who encounter a list arranged by recommended food pairings is to take a step back, quickly scan the list, and see if you agree with most of the pairings. If you do, it probably means the list's been well put together, and you should either (1) go ahead with one of the place's suggestions, or (2) break the rules anyway—and by that I mean choose a wine from a different category, based on the wine and food guidelines you learned in Chapter 6. In other words, mix it up like the hip taster you are!

Wild Cards

Because people—especially restaurant people—are inherently creative creatures, you should also expect to happen upon lists prepared according to what I like to call "wild card" methods. These lists run the gamut from inventive and inspired to downright bizarre and nonsensical. Some of the more interesting versions include categories like "Weird and Unusual" selections, wines made by young and/or innovative producers, award-winning wines, old and rare wines, and newly released wines. The possibilities are endless, as are the opportunities they can afford to discover the new and unique.

Sizing Up the Quality of a Restaurant's List

Now that we've talked about the different kinds of lists you can expect to encounter, how do you know whether a list is a good one? Contrary to popular belief, the best restaurant wine lists aren't necessarily the most lengthy. In fact, some of the best lists I've ever seen are on the shorter side and contain, rather than a book-length selection of options, a mere handful of really good wines. These are the well-edited, easy-to-use lists that you'll encounter, if you're lucky, at forward-thinking restaurants that understand that quality trumps quantity every time.

No matter what its length, a restaurant's list is probably a good one if it contains at least a few good sparkling wines, whites of varying weights—but especially the crisp, un-oaked, food-friendly variety—ditto for reds, and at least a couple of dessert wines. And although I prefer lists that include wines from around the world, lists that focus on wines from a single region *can* manage to represent adequate stylistic breadth if the list's author has worked very diligently.

Many restaurants in California, for example, feature exclusively California wine. Based on what we know about California's warm climate, this means that it can be challenging for diners at these spots to find wines with adequate acidity to partner with difficult dishes, like those with lots of spice. In these instances the list's author can overcome the problem by including wines from cooler parts of California, like northerly Sonoma and Mendocino counties, whose wines tend to have higher acidity, or reach for wines with naturally high acidity, like Sauvignon Blanc and Pinot Noir.

The Money Issue: How Much Is Too Much?

Restaurants are businesses and, accordingly, they aim to make a profit. Unfortunately, a disproportionate amount of this profit often comes from wine and liquor sales, due to the hefty markups that are common for these items in restaurants. Generally, restaurants mark up wines two to three times over the standard retail price you'd expect to pay for the same bottles in a wine shop. They justify this based on the additional storage, stemware, and service costs associated with keeping and serving the wine, although I rarely find that these additional costs justify the—sometimes exorbitantly high—markups.

To determine if you're being ripped off, try to find a familiar bottle on the list and mentally calculate the markup. Is it at the higher end of the markup scale, like three times, or even more? If so, an unscrupulous owner or manager is eating your lunch, figuratively speaking. On the other hand, you may discover that the establishment has marked up the wine to the lower end of the scale, which means it's betting that it will sell more wine with these lower prices. Growing numbers of restaurants are embracing this philosophy of less is more when it comes to markups, something that's music to my ears.

The 411 on BYO Etiquette

After all this talk about markups, bringing your own bottle is probably starting to sound pretty good. BYO is a great alternative to ordering a bottle off a restaurant's list, but there are a couple of rules of thumb that are important to keep in mind when doing so:

• Never bring a bottle that's on the restaurant's list.

This is inconsiderate to the establishment, as its proprietors would make more money if they sold you the same bottle from their own cellar. You can avoid this awkward situation by calling ahead or consulting the wine list online (if available). Many restaurants will refuse to open bottles that they also sell.

• Call ahead to make sure you *can* bring your own.

Some restaurants don't allow customers to bring their own wine. Spare yourself the burden of lugging around a bottle all night by calling ahead.

• Inquire about the corkage fee.

Ask what the corkage fee is in advance. This is what a restaurant charges guests for the privilege of bringing their own. It would be a shame to discover when the bill arrives that this fee is absurdly high! Depending on the place, you should expect to pay from ten to thirty dollars.
(Note: Some restos offer free corkage on certain nights of the week—a great thing to know!)

• Don't bring a mediocre bottle.

There's nothing more frustrating than for a restaurant of a certain caliber to discover that a guest has brought a widely available wine anyone can pluck off a retailer's shelf for twelve dollars. Although economics may play a role in your decision to BYO, the point of bringing your own should at least *appear* to be that the bottle's special in some way.

• Offer your server or sommelier a taste.

Because you've exercised the privilege of bringing your own, it's a gesture of politeness to the establishment to offer whoever is serving you a taste of your special wine. Particularly if the bottle is old or rare, this is a nice gesture.

Step 2: Making Your Selection

Now that you've sized up the list, it's time to choose your wine. You'll need to consider a few key factors in making your decision:

- how many courses you'll have
- what you and your companions are eating
- your budget
- the occasion

These are all pretty straightforward considerations, but let's take a closer look at them to make sure you feel fully prepared.

The Multicourse Meal: How to Deal

If you're having a multicourse meal, meaning you're probably starting with appetizers, you might begin with a starter-appropriate light- to medium-bodied white or a light red, if you're with a red wine–only kind of group. From there, you'll want to choose wines for subsequent courses that increase in weight along with the food, of course taking into account any particularly "difficult" qualities (e.g., excessive saltiness or sweetness) in the dishes your companions have ordered. And, if possible, it's always a good idea to preorder wines for subsequent courses so you'll have a better shot at their arriving at the appropriate time.

The Food:
How Hard Does Your Wine Have to Work?

If you're *not* having multiple courses, or you just want to choose a single wine to enjoy throughout your meal, consider opting for a wine that straddles different styles. The best of these is an Old World Chardonnay of a not-too-oaky nature, especially from France, due to its medium body and flexible flavor profile. Some Chardonnays from

California's cool Sonoma region are also good bets, as are versions coming out of cool Western Australia. These mellow Chards will work adequately with most starters; pastas in white or neutral sauces; and fish, chicken, and some not-too-heavy meat dishes, like pork. Dry Rieslings and Pinot Blancs are great options as well. If your companions are interested in a "bigger" wine, and white's a must, opt for Viognier, the "big white" that appeals to red drinkers, too. If red's your ticket, Pinot Noir works well for groups because it shares Chardonnay's flexibility with a broad array of dishes.

Take Advantage of Small Pours

Savvy restaurants and wine bars are increasingly offering small pours, or "tastes," in response to patrons' growing interest in trying more and different kinds of wines. Small pours are great ways for guests to get over the hurdle of trying something new, as the commitment factor is low—most small pours clock in at around two ounces, about a third of a normal glass of wine.

Besides small pours, innovative establishments are also offering flights, or groups of small tasting-sized pours, usually organized around some sort of theme. These flights are a great way to try several new wines at once, all with the low commitment threshold of a small pour. If you're feeling really adventurous, ask your bartender or server if he or she can customize a flight for you. Now *that's* hip.

Your Budget: Anxiety Overload

Unless you just got your bonus or came into an unexpectedly large inheritance (lucky you!), chances are good that your wine budget when dining out is a lot like mine: not huge. And there's nothing wrong with that, although it brings up a key catalyst for the anxiety so many people feel over ordering wine in restaurants—the money issue. In the absence of a deep knowledge of wine, many diners understandably look to price as an indicator of the quality of the wines on the list. "The more expensive the bottle," they reason, "the better chance it'll be good, and I won't look like a buffoon who just ordered a bad bottle for my friends/family/coworkers." Like I said, understandably a tough situation!

But, if a wine is on a reputable restaurant's list, it should be a good option for you and your companions, no matter the price. When a wine appears on a restaurant's list, it's been selected—hopefully with great care and attention—from a pool of other possible wines. Usually it's been singled out from at least a few dozen alternatives and, in the case of restaurants with really great wine programs, from hundreds of other wines that didn't make the cut. And as with making movies, making up a wine list is as much about what's left on the cutting room floor, so to speak, as what winds up in the final picture. Don't allow unscrupulous servers or sommeliers to push you toward more expensive bottles if you're uncomfortable paying more!

Special-Occasion Wines: Stepping It Up

Now, there *are* certain occasions when it makes sense to splurge on a special bottle, assuming it's in your budget. These are the big occasions—birthdays, engagements, weddings, anniversaries, graduations, promotions, and the like. In these instances, choosing a suitably festive wine can go a long way toward heightening the drama of the event. The reason is that wine service, with its timeless sense of formality and importance, is in and of itself a dramatic event. It just *feels* like a big deal to have a bottle of bubbly popped tableside, or an older red decanted before drinking. Like I said, instant drama!

The hands-down best special-occasion wines are, without

a doubt, vintage or prestige cuvée Champagnes. You'll recall from Chapter 4 that these are the hundred-dollar-and-
up rarities such as Dom Pérignon and Cristal that are made
in limited quantities from only the best grapes coming out
of Champagne's vineyards. Besides these, other big occasion wines include mature reds from Bordeaux, Burgundy,
and, increasingly, Italy's top red wine regions, Piedmont
(for Barolo) and Tuscany (for Brunello di Montalcino).
Some cult California Cabs also make great special occasion
wines, as do other limited-production bottlings of outstanding mature wines from around the world. At the end
of the day, though, if you think a wine—any wine, for that
matter—is special, then that's the only green light you need
to proceed.

Hip to Know: The Power of BYO

The only way the drama of ordering a so-called
special occasion wine can be topped, in my opinion, is by bringing *your own* special occasion–caliber
wine, ideally something you put some thought
into and sought out specifically for the occasion.
Those who do this will score serious points for
their ingenuity and thoughtfulness!

Step 3: Placing Your Order

Congratulations, you're finally ready to order some booze.
Depending on the particular restaurant and its staffing and
service protocol, you'll be presenting your order either to
your server or to a wine waiter/sommelier type. In some
restaurants the sommelier is there only to present and serve
the wine, not to take the order. It totally depends on the
place, and, like I said, it varies widely.

No matter what, the person taking your order will address whomever he or she perceives to be the host, or decision maker, at the table and ask you if you're ready to order the wine. As a young female, I'm frequently in the position of needing to speak up at this point if I'm ordering the wine, as the server has invariably addressed the question to a (usually) male but (inevitably) older person at the table! No matter: You just speak up at this point and say, "I'll be ordering the wine this evening," or whatever else you need to say to get the point across.

When You Know What You Want

If you've already made your selection, all you need to do at this point is communicate your order to the server. You can either announce your selection out loud or, if you'd prefer to be more discreet, you can just point to your selection on the list. This is also a good time to make any specific requests related to the wine, such as the order of service (if you're ordering more than one wine), additional glasses, decanting, or the timing of the service (don't hesitate to tell your server when you'd like the wines to arrive!).

If you'll be ordering additional bottles for a multicourse meal, it's also a good idea to place those orders at this time, so that the staff has ample time to prepare them and, hopefully, serve them at the same time as their complementary courses. The reason I reiterate this is because restaurants with extensive wine collections and/or older wines will often take longer to retrieve bottles, since many of them are located in remote sections of a cellar or wine locker. Further, many older red wines require decanting to remove sediment prior to serving, and decanting—as you might imagine—takes time. Besides all this, preordering all your wine means you get the anxiety-inducing task over with at the outset and can relax for the rest of your meal!

Asking for a Taste

Many restaurants are glad to give guests free tastes of wines they're considering ordering, particularly if these wines are availble by the glass. The reason is that wines being poured by the glass are usually already open and, as a result, it's easy for servers to pour out a small amount for your consideration. I'll often ask for tastes at casual places like wine bars or while at the bar in a restaurant, while waiting to be seated. This can be a great way to help narrow down your choices without commiting to an entire glass, and it also comes in handy if you think you might order a bottle of the same wine later for your table.

When You Need Help

Now, the tricky part. Few things strike fear more deeply into the hearts of diners than the prospect of asking a sommelier or server for help with a wine order. Fortunately, I've found that people in the wine service business tend to be kindly types who would rather help you find a suitable selection than overcharge you. When you consider that being a sommelier is far from the most lucrative profession, and often involves incessant schlepping of cases of wine during the day followed by long, late nights in a restaurant, you start to see that these people are really in the job because they love what they do. And although many sommeliers and servers are incentivized when it comes to wine sales, some of the more enlightened folks realize that they'll sell more if they recommend bottles suitable to their clientele, who are then more likely to place additional orders (and become repeat customers, I might add).

So, back to asking for help. We've established that you

probably want to ask for help but are worried that you'll be overcharged or browbeaten into an odd and possibly unpleasant selection if you do. These feelings are normal, but you need to get over them! Like I said, most sommeliers and servers really *do* want to help, and many also sense your anxiety and will do whatever they can to make you feel more comfortable.

The Tip-off

The tip-off gives servers and sommeliers the opportunity to help you discreetly. If price is your main criterion, simply point to the prices next to a couple of wines you're comfortable with and say, "I'm looking for something like this." If the server makes a suggestion that you'd like to hear more about, ask for more information. Totally acceptable questions include "Will that work well with what we're all having?" and "Can you recommend a red instead?" You can also use the tip-off method if you'd like to give your server a different framework (e.g., grape variety, region) to work within. Just point to several wines you're considering and let your server know you're choosing between them. Can he or she make a suggestion? There are no wrong questions. The only thing *you* can do wrong is to not speak up and get the information you need to feel good about your selection.

If you'd feel more comfortable asking for help behind the scenes, it's totally acceptable (and smart, in my book) to call ahead and arrange to speak with the sommelier, restaurant manager, or proprietor about your needs before your meal. This is a bit time consuming, but it can come in handy for high-stress dining situations, such as work-related meals where you'd rather not have to make your selection on the spot in front of your guests. It's also a good idea when you'd just like to eliminate the pressure of the wine order from the flow of your meal; this might be the case on special occasions, like a first date (with or without a sommelier).

Whatever your reason for calling ahead, I can tell you that most sommeliers, managers, and proprietors are impressed when diners are this proactive about their wine selections. It's also flattering for these folks, who get to do what they love most without the extra pressure of the sometimes awkward tableside order.

Hip to Know: Check Out the List Online

In the past few years I've been thrilled to discover that many restaurants are taking their menus and wine lists online, posting them on their Web sites along with their contact information, hours of operation, and the like. This is great news, as it affords diners the opportunity to get comfortable with their food and wine options in advance.

Besides the benefit of giving diners more time to noodle over their ordering possibilities, online menus and wine lists also provide a lower intensity alternative for seeking out help before a meal. Instead of calling the establishment to seek guidance in making a wine selection, those with access to online lists can pursue all sorts of means to make a great choice—they can call wine-savvy friends, consult a favorite retail clerk, or cross-reference wine and food pairing recommendations like those found in this book. This is the DIY method, and it's my favorite way to choose wine in advance!

Tasting Time

Once your wine arrives you'll need to taste it and give your approval—in other words, you've got to *accept* it before it's then poured around the table for your guests. What you're looking for here are any flaws in the wine. You may recall from Chapter 2 that if the wine smells at all like cardboard, chemicals, vinegar, or pretty much anything else excessively unpleasant, chances are good that it's flawed. And you don't even need to go so far as tasting the wine to identify these things—they're usually abundantly clear to the nose.

Sending a Bottle Back

In these instances you should politely tell your server that you believe the bottle is bad. You aren't obligated to identify the flaw (indeed, even some wine professionals have trouble determining exactly what's wrong with bad bottles); instead, it's just important that you speak confidently and ask that the bottle be replaced. Thanks to the fairly ubiquitous "the customer is always right" mentality in the United States, you'll usually find that expressing your opinion about a flawed wine is all you need to do to successfully send it back.

In the rare instances when you *do* encounter friction, your best defense is a good offense: Ask the server or sommelier to taste the wine herself. By engaging the server in this way you actively involve her in your decision and will usually find that she respectfully declines your offer and brings out a new bottle. If for any reason your server seems fixed on your keeping the wine (a horrific display of customer service, in my opinion), ask to speak to the manager. I think you'll find you get your new bottle in no time.

Wine Service No-nos:
What to Watch for and How to Cope

Occasionally—okay, more often than I care to relate—you'll encounter subpar wine service out in the world. This happens for a number of reasons, chief among them that wine is served in a vast array of establishments, all of which have varying degrees of knowledge about the stuff and a correspondingly varied interest in making their wine programs top-notch. Below are a few of the more glaring examples of the worst wine service offenses and suggestions on how to cope when you encounter them.

• Temperature issues

Most white table wines should be served cool, but not just-out-of-the-fridge cold, as excessive chill masks the nuances in white wine. If your white is served too cold, tell your server. Occasionally they can warm it up a little by running it under some warm water in the kitchen. Lighter reds like Pinot Noir, on the other hand, are best served cooler than room temperature. If your red's too warm, ask for an ice bucket. If your server looks at you like you're crazy, take it out of his tip.

• Gargantuan pours

After everything we've learned about how important smelling a wine is to the tasting experience, it should come as no surprise that a major pet peeve of mine is when a server pours a glass of wine all the way up to the brim, leaving you no room to swirl and stoke all those wonderful vapors found in wine. If this happens to you, ask that your wine be served in a bigger glass; if there are no larger glasses available, ask for another glass of the same size and pour half of your wine into it, essentially creating the same effect.

• Cheap stemware

This rant depends on the establishment: Clearly, a pizza parlor shouldn't be expected to carry nice glassware. But, if you're in a spot where you're splurging on a high-end meal and nice wine, that place has an obligation to serve your wine in stemware that matches the caliber of the wine. Good glasses are made from thin crystal blown in ideal shapes that enhance your tasting experience. Because nice stemware is expensive to buy and store, some restaurants keep some on hand but don't provide it unless it's specifically requested. So, if you don't think your glass measures up to your wine, ask for one that does.

- Slow service

    No matter what or how you order, I can't emphasize enough how important it is to ask for exactly what you want when it comes to wine service—and this includes timing. As a paying customer, it's your right to receive precise and thoughtful service. So if you find yourself halfway through your first course and your wine's still not there, speak up. There's nothing worse than something like bad service coming between you and the good stuff.

When You'd Rather Dine In

Does all this talk about bad service make you want to grab a bottle at your local wine shop and order in? It's no wonder! Wine at home has all the benefits of wine out in the world, with fewer distractions and no bill at the end of the night. Chapter 8 includes tips for storing, serving, and enjoying wine at home, plus advice on how to throw fabulous wine parties in your own pad. So read on, because it's party time!

Party in a Box—Literally

After years of buildup and giddy anticipation, it finally happened not long ago: I got my first apartment on my own. It's a glorified studio with a separate office offering sweeping views of San Francisco and the bay, and I knew it was "the one" from the moment I first stepped inside. Never mind that it's a fourth-floor walk-up with no laundry, no dishwasher, and no parking (not to mention that the floor slants): I think it's absolutely perfect.

But its tiny size presents a problem when it comes to entertaining. Assuming I can coax guests up the steep hill where I live to then brave the many steps leading to my door, I've got to be extremely creative when it comes to fitting them into my little place comfortably. And even though the "bedroom" is practically in the living room, it hardly seems appropriate to serve cocktails to friends while they lounge on my bed—this ain't *that* kind of party!

But with a little planning and space-saving ingenuity, I usually manage to carry off a perfectly respectable get-together. And, it being a get-together of mine, the party invariably involves wine—usually lots of it, music of a certain decibel level, and some really great displays of revelry (which I won't disclose here for the safety and anonymity of my guests). All this, I might add, within the confines of an apartment smaller than some folks' walk-in closets.

At the end of the day a party's success has a lot more to do with your attitude and readiness for fun than anything as limiting as a space constraint. But it can still help to have a plan for some of the trickier aspects of party planning, especially those related to hosting a wine-themed gathering. Read on for everything you need to know about throwing a fabulous wine tasting in your own pad (no matter its size), as well as advice on wine tools and gadgets, storage units, stemware, and techniques for serving the good stuff.

I'll leave the displays of revelry up to you and your guests.

Wine at Home
Storage and Must-Have Wine Gear

The Setup: Stemware and Service Temps

Keeping a few key items on hand and learning some basic rules of thumb about serving wine can dramatically improve your wine-at-home experience.

Stemware Made Simple

While drinking from high-quality wineglasses like those made by celebrated Austrian glassmaker Riedel will improve your wine experience, drinking from run-of-the-mill stems won't necessarily detract from it. Especially for parties and large groups, using generic wineglasses or the faddish new stemless versions is completely acceptable and practical, especially given the sometimes prohibitive cost of higher-end stemware. And as a result of wine's growing popularity in the United States, a number of retailers and warehouse stores have begun selling both types of glasses (both high-end and more generic versions) in bulk, making it more affordable than ever to stock up on a good number of glasses for these occasions.

And unless you're serving sangria, it's preferable to drink wine from a glass with a bowl, whether it's attached to a stem or not. The reason is that the bulbous shape of a wineglass allows aromas to waft up and collect in the upper portion of the glass, where your nose can take them all in. Tumblers and water glasses are ill fit for the job due to their tendency to slant gradually *outward,* which allows the aromas to escape. Also, they make it almost impossible to swirl the wine, which is what really promotes the release of all of these great scents! So, if you've gone to the effort and expense of buying nice wine for your guests (or just for yourself!), then do everyone a favor and serve it in suitably bulbous glasses.

Let's Give It Up for the Stems

There's a practical reason why many a wineglass comes equipped with a stem: It's where we're supposed to hang on to the thing. Because our hands are greasy, holding a glass by the bowl leaves behind telltale fingerprints that can look pretty gross. Besides this ick factor, our hands are hot little transmitters of body heat, and if you've gone to the trouble of serving your wine at an ideal temperature (read on for help with this), it's a shame to then ratchet it up several degrees simply because you're holding it by the bowl. Stemless wineglasses fall prey to both of these evils, which is why they're best used for more casual affairs. In other words, if you're splurging on a '61 Château d'Yquem (duh-kem) from Sauternes, reach for a stem.

Whites Versus Reds: A Tale of Two Glasses

Generally, red wines are most enhanced by large glasses that give them lots of room to come to life (cue vocab: breathe). Most white wines, on the other hand, don't need as much stoking to show off their full aromatic and flavor potential, and as a result they're usually served in smaller glasses. Technically speaking, good white-wine glasses hold at least eight to twelve ounces of liquid, while red-wine glasses ideally hold from twelve to twenty-four ounces, and sometimes more.

Hip to Know: When One Glass Will Do the Trick

I prefer to serve guests both whites and reds in a single large glass (as you'll recall, I don't have a dishwasher, so this is a welcome relief at the end of the night!). When I host a wine tasting, I set out a spittoon or "dump bucket," as I like to call it, and encourage folks to dump in whatever wine they'd rather not finish. This way, guests can continue to use the same glass throughout the evening. The best glasses for this strategy are those of at least medium size—twelve ounces—which work with both whites and reds.

Mr. Big Glass

If and when you're ready to step it up to fancier glasses, I recommend starting out by investing in some of a versatile style that will work with both white and red wines. If you've done any research on the subject you're probably aware that some luxe glassmakers carry dozens of different glasses, each of which has been fine-tuned to suit a different kind of wine (e.g., Chardonnay, Pinot Noir, Zinfandel). While I'd love to have every different kind of stem out there, an extensive glass collection just doesn't make sense for me right now.

So instead, I use Riedel Bordeaux-style stems for all of my everyday wine drinking. They're big enough to coax out the complex aromas of reds but they also work with whites. And, most important, they're made of fine crystal, a substance that's been proven—along with the size and shape of a glass—to enhance the way we perceive aromas and flavors in wine.

Quick Tip. German glassmaker Spiegelau makes nice stems as well, for a bit less than Riedel's.

I'll Take the Hundred-Dollar Glass, Thanks

Besides making a whole slew of glasses for different grape varieties and blends, Riedel makes a super-high-end "Sommelier" series of stems that retail for around a hundred bucks a pop. That's right, one hundred dollars for *one glass*. They're made by traditional Austrian glassmaking methods, including a process involving mouth-blowing the glass into molds. Now *that's* what I call stepping it up.

Don't Forget the Flutes!

Besides your standard wineglasses, it's a great idea to invest in some Champagne flutes. The reason is that bubbly wines are ideally suited to these tall, narrow glasses that facilitate the upward streaming of the CO_2 bubbles sparkling wines give off. And besides this, tall and narrow flutes have the additional benefit of showing bubble streams off to their best advantage. There are few things more satisfying to me than watching a crew of really lively Champagne bubbles course upward in an elegant flute. Maybe it sounds like a cheap thrill, but I dig it every time.

Temperature

Wines' complex aromas and flavors reveal themselves fully to lucky tasters when they're served at ideal temperatures. Unfortunately, there's a yin to this yang: Serve wines at imprecise temps and you're likely to miss most of the show. This is because wine—as you've probably gathered by now—is an incredibly delicate thing. Not only is it susceptible to all sorts of flaws and spoilage traps, but it also trots out all of its true colors only when stored and served *just so*. And, just as there are many different styles of wine, there are a correspondingly varied number of ideal temperatures for serving it.

Are you annoyed yet? I am! It's understandably frustrating to try to keep track of all of these prerequisites to enjoying the good stuff, and it's also why I've laid out for you in this chapter, as clearly as possible, some helpful pointers for doing just that.

Please Pass the Thermometer . . . *NOT!*

I don't know about you, but I don't recall the last time I actually took a wine's temperature. There are gadgets for doing this, but I don't own any of them. Instead, I've just learned through experience what feels right to me when I grab ahold of a bottle I'm about to serve. A good point of reference is refrigerator temperature, which for most households clocks in around 35° to 40° Fahrenheit. When you consider that most whites should be poured about 15° to 20° warmer (around 50° to 55°), and most reds 25° to 30° warmer (around 60° to 65°), you begin to see that it's not terrifically tough to make an educated guess.

Sparklers and Whites

Most white and sparkling wines are best drunk "cold," but just-out-of-the-fridge cold is too chilly. This is because the volatile compounds in wine can't adequately come to life at such low temperatures. Instead, serve these wines a little warmer. The better quality the wine, the more of a consideration this becomes: Simple, crisp white wines have fewer aromatic and flavor goodies to show off, and as a result can be served quite cool, but the best sparkling wines, such as vintage Champagne, and complex whites, including good Chardonnay, are particularly sensitive to excessive chill.

Quick Tip. If you've got wine in your refrigerator, take out crisp whites fifteen minutes before drinking, and reds and more complex wines twenty to thirty minutes before.

Mask the Ick with a Little Ice

Occasionally, although I'd rather not admit it, I find myself in the unlucky situation of having no choice but to quaff practically unpalatable wine. This usually happens at big events like business receptions, where one or two subpar wines are the only booze options available to guests. If you find yourself in this situation, opt for a white (if you've got the choice) and plunk a couple of ice cubes into your glass to get it really cold. Excessive chill masks the aromas and flavors in wine. Sometimes that can be a very, very good thing.

Reds

Although it's rarely discussed, many red wines are actually best when drunk slightly chilled. This is often the case for light- to medium-bodied reds with sturdy acidity, such as many a Pinot Noir, French Gamay (from Beaujolais), and Barbera. The reason is that when poured at room temperature, these wines' acidity tastes unappealingly astringent, much as the acidity in a white wine would if it were served at—shudder—room temperature.

An easy and practical way to get these reds to the right temp is to stick them in the fridge for about thirty minutes before you're ready to serve them. Fuller-bodied reds such as Brunello di Montalcino and Cabernet Sauvignon will also benefit from a slight chill; give these bigger guys fifteen minutes in your fridge. If you've got your wine stored in a temperature-controlled cabinet or minifridge, the same logic applies in reverse: Take the wines *out* fifteen to thirty minutes before serving. Presto!

When to Get Over the Grease

You can easily warm up a wine by cupping your hands around the bowl of your glass for a few minutes. Our hands transmit body heat, something that can come in handy if your wine has gotten a little too much chill. This process will invariably leave behind a few fingerprints on your glass, but it's worth the trade-off. I'll take a greasy glass full of delicious wine at the perfect temperature over a pristinely clean but lifeless, cold glass any day.

Sweeties

Most dessert wines are best served chilled. The degree of chilliness depends on the quality and style of the sweet wine, with the simpler stuff requiring more chill and the better stuff, such as good quality nobly rotten wines like Sauternes, a little less. Strong wines like port can take a little more warmth.

Recommended Service Temps

While you shouldn't keep yourself up at night worrying about whether the last Pinot you served clocked in at 62° versus 58° Fahrenheit, it can be helpful to have a breakdown of ideal wine service temps. So with no further ado:

Champagne and sparkling wines: 45°F
Still whites: 50°F to 55°F
Fine Champagne and full-bodied whites:
    52°F to 60°F
Dessert wines: 58°F to 62°F
Light-bodied still reds: 58°F to 60°F
Bigger-bodied still reds: 60°F to 65°F
Port and other strong wines: 62°F to 65°F

Author's Picks:
Crowd-Pleasing Party Wines

A handful of wines sure to win over even your pickiest guests, without putting a dent in your savings:

Annie's Lane Riesling, Clare Valley, Australia
Casa Lapostolle "Cuvée Alexandre" Merlot,
    Colchagua Valley, Chile
Marqués de Cáceres Crianza Red, Rioja, Spain
Matua Valley Sauvignon Blanc, Marlborough,
    New Zealand
Saintsbury "Garnet" Pinot Noir, Carneros,
    California
Sonoma-Cutrer "Russian River Ranches"
    Chardonnay, Sonoma, California

Storing Your Wine: What You Need to Know

Given what you now know about wine's delicate nature, you can probably imagine that there are a few things that can spell disaster when it comes to storage. This is why wine storage is best explained in the context of "don'ts" rather than "dos."

Don't

- **Allow your wine to be exposed to too much light.** The best storage spots are completely dark, but a relatively dark spot like a closet or under a stairwell will do the trick. The UV rays in sunlight, in particular, wreak havoc on exposed bottles.
- **Store bottles in high-vibration areas.** Wine is most happy when kept perfectly still, although occasional movement won't do it in completely. Just don't leave wine next to your refrigerator, hot water heater, or other vibration-prone device.
- **Store wine near strong odors.** Because cork is porous, particularly strong odors such as paint and detergent can actually get into the bottle and do damage to your wine. Pee-yew!
- **Let the good stuff get too hot.** Long-term storage of fine wine calls for precise temperature consideration (ideally, 55° Fahrenheit), but for bottles you intend to knock back in the near future you need only protect them from excessive heat. The upper limit is about 75° Fahrenheit. Also keep in mind that significant temperature fluctuation isn't good.
- **Let the cork dry out.** Storing wine bottles on their sides allows the wine to remain in contact with the cork and keep it moist and plump. Without this moisture the cork will dry out and shrink up, allowing excessive amounts of oxygen to creep in and ruin your wine. Adequate humidity—about 70 percent, ideally—is also necessary to

keep the cork plump and moist, but you need to worry about this only for long-term storage.

Wine Storage Options

For those of you who live in spaces that don't facilitate storing wine (like a tiny fourth-floor walk-up in San Francisco), or for those who simply don't have a desire to do so, there are some simple things you can do to make sure your wine stays in decent shape until you're ready to drink it. If you have the space *and* inclination to save wine for the longer term, you've got a lot more options for keeping your good stuff in fine shape.

Wine and Refrigerators: Proceed with Caution

Most home refrigerators make adequate storage places for your wine *in the short term.* Try not to leave wine of any value in the fridge for longer than several weeks, as bottles start to suffer from the lack of moisture in most fridges after that (remember that humidity is needed to keep corks from shrinking and the wine from oxidizing). And the fridge is definitely the *wrong* place for red and white wines of any value that are expected to evolve over time in storage; besides the humidity issue, the temperature in your fridge is too low for wine's development.

Storing Wine: The Low-Fi Version

If you're like me and don't have a proper cellar, there are some rules of thumb you're best off observing so you don't wind up with vinegar where there was once a decent bottle of wine. The first is to have realistic expectations about your wine storage options. If your "cellar" is a cool, dark interior closet, then you're in good shape to keep a few bottles or cases of average to good quality wine in there that are meant to be drunk within a few months. I definitely don't recommend keeping anything that's meant for long-term storage (as in years) in a closet, because, unless you're living in a remarkably cool climate without indoor heating, it's almost certainly warmer in your closet than the recommended 55° Fahrenheit that's best for long-term wine storage.

In the shorter term, storing wine on its side in a rack in your kitchen or living room is totally acceptable, just so long as you keep it out of direct sunlight. Your fridge is a good short-term option for storing wines of all styles as well, but your timeline here is even shorter—just a matter of weeks before the fridge's lack of humidity will begin to take a toll on your good stuff. Ultimately, there's no reason apartment dwellers and folks not inclined to invest in a cellar or wine-cooling unit can't enjoy good wine. You just need to drink up any wine you store soon, and keep restocking as needed.

Storing Wine: The Hi-Fi Version

If you've got a cool basement or cellar in your home (you lucky dog!) you're ready to keep all kinds of different wines on hand, for however long you plan to live there. In these instances you still need to heed the "don'ts" I already listed—meaning you need to make sure your space has an adequately cool temperature, sufficiently high humidity, and low light, and is free of excessive vibration. But once you've made sure of these factors, you're in good shape to store wine for both short- and long-term periods. And special devices that regulate temperature and humidity in wine cellar–type environments are widely available, in the event that you need a helping hand creating your ideal home wine-storage environment.

Cellar conditions can also be mimicked by wine-storage units, or "cabinets," as they're often called. These refrigerator-like containers hold anywhere from a half-dozen to hundreds of bottles of wine and allow you to control the temperature at which your bottles are kept (usually between 50° and 65°). I highly recommend purchasing one of these if you're looking for an intermediate, portable, and extremely efficient way to keep your good stuff in tip-top shape (units start around $100). Cabinets as well as temperature- and humidity-control devices are widely available through wine accessory retailers like the Wine Enthusiast (800-356-8644, or wineenthusiast.com).

Goods and Gadgetry

Having a decent set of wine service tools on hand is mission critical for anyone with plans to serve wine at home. After all, there's nothing more frustrating than botching one of the essential prerequisites for enjoying wine (like getting the cork out of the bottle), especially in front of guests. Turns out that unfortunate incidents like this can often be attributed as much to a lousy corkscrew as to the skill of the remover! Happily, folks with the right wine service tools need not fear this sort of embarrassment. Read on for the 411 on the best screws and other tools.

Corkscrew Me

My favorite tool for getting wine open quickly and cleanly is the simple, widely available waiter's corkscrew, which takes its name from its popularity with the folks who serve us the good stuff in restaurants and bars. The waiter's corkscrew has a simple Teflon "worm" (the spiral prong that you stick into the cork), a lever for removing the cork, and a little knife that's used for cutting the foil off the top of the bottle. The easiest-to-use versions have what's called a "double lever" that facilitates the biggest range of motion (with the least effort, I might add) for removing the cork. Even better, waiter's corkscrews are cheap: You can often find them for as little as five dollars.

Other options in cork removal include the straightforward Screwpull corkscrew, the ubiquitous "winged" corkscrew—which I don't recommend, due to its tendency to maul corks—and the Ah-So cork puller. The Screwpull is a great alternative to the waiter's corkscrew and requires less brute strength (twisting takes the place of lever pulling), and the Ah-So is a double-pronged device that's helpful for removing old or crumbly corks but can be tough with new and very well stuck-in corks. Avoid winged corkscrews (the ones with the levers on both sides that rise up like a butterfly as the cork comes out) at all costs, unless you want to be "that" guy or gal who couldn't get the cork out of the bottle.

A discussion of corkscrews wouldn't be complete without a few words on the ubiquitous Rabbit corkscrew, a pricey black-and-chrome number that seems to function as much as status symbol as wine tool. Why the gripes? The Rabbit and its many knockoffs weigh in at around a hefty two pounds each and require an advanced degree to operate (or at least a similarly hefty manual). Once you *do* figure out how they work, Rabbits can be quite handy—they do, as retailers promise, remove corks in a single, nearly effortless pull. Still, I find them a waste of space and awkward to operate because of their heft. And although lighter, more streamlined versions of this one-pull technology are now available, their astronomical price tags (some are as much as $100 each) make them impractical for all but the best-funded tasters.

Fun with Foil Cutters

If you've ever opened more than a few bottles of wine at one time you'll appreciate the speed and efficiency of a foil cutter. Foil cutters are mostly round devices made of plastic with inlaid blades and are designed to fit over the top of a bottle. You squeeze and twist them and—voilà!—the top of the foil cap comes off in a single clean movement, leaving the cork exposed and ready for you to remove. As you might imagine, foil cutters are terrifically handy for parties and other times when you'll be opening a number of bottles. And while the knife on a waiter's corkscrew can also be used to remove the foil around the top of a bottle, a foil cutter will make a quicker, cleaner cut every time.

Hip Tools: Must-Have Wine Gear

- Built NY neoprene wine tote, especially in a cool color (camouflage, anyone?). *The* way to carry your wine when BYO is a must, these stylish wine totes are made from neoprene, the stuff wet suits are made of. BuiltNY.com.
- Good, compact wine fridge. Why get in on the good stuff only to risk its going bad? Plus, the best coolers look very chic, even in the smallest spaces. Wineenthusiast.com.
- Set of reliable wine stoppers, especially those from Vacu Vin. The same logic applies here: If you're going to bother opening a bottle of the good stuff, shouldn't you take good care of your leftovers? Amazon.com.
- Pedrini chrome-plated Champagne stopper. Even cooler than popping the cork on some bubbly is when it keeps its fizz for another glass tomorrow. Plus, this is *so* easy to use, so why not? Target.com.
- Riedel "O" stemless wineglasses. I love how cool these look, and they're less likely to get knocked over by the occasionally errant elbow (or enthusiastic sipper)! Wineenthusiast.com.

Spittoons to the Rescue

I know it sounds silly to say that spittoons can rescue you from anything, but in fact they've been known to save many a taster from a raging hangover. Basically buckets where you dump or spit wine you don't plan to drink, spittoons are good things to put out at parties so that your guests can relieve themselves of any unwanted booze. You can find them in inexpensive plastic or metal versions at some specialty wine shops and lots of larger wine retail chains, although in a pinch an ice bucket or similar container will do the trick just fine. Spittoons are especially helpful if you're hosting a true tasting, at which guests will be sampling many wines, not all of which they'll want to finish. They also come in handy anytime you're entertaining guests who'll be using a single glass throughout the night.

Decanters, Their Doppelgängers, and How to Use 'Em

Decanting is one of those mysterious wine service techniques that can seem uppity and unnecessary to the uninitiated. Well, allow me to initiate you: Decanting is neither uppity nor unnecessary, and can be, on many occasions, the extra step that takes an average-seeming wine to glorious new heights. Besides that, decanting also removes sediment from older wines, something that's handy if you'd rather not drink particles with your Pétrus. Also worth noting is the fact that the two reasons you decant wine—to aerate it and to remove sediment from it—are rarely *both* required for the same wine.

Decanting for Aeration

Aeration is what's often called for when young red wines seem overly tannic and lacking in fruit (cue vocab: closed). Pouring a closed wine into a decanter or similar pitcher-like receptacle stimulates the mixing of the wine with oxygen, essentially simulating the effect of bottle maturation (which, you may recall, over time softens the tannins and encourages the development of a wine's bouquet).

So, just as wine benefits from the slow influx of oxygen through porous cork over years in a cellar, a young wine can benefit tremendously from the quick shock of oxygen that occurs when you pour it into a bigger container and swish it around prior to serving. For maximum aeration, pour the wine back and forth several times between two decanters. This process—known as double decantation—has been known to transform simple, young reds into much more layered, complex wines. If you don't have two decanters, any two large, clean containers will do. I've even been known to use flower vases!

Quick Tip. Besides swishing the wine around in the decanter to stimulate this beneficial mixing of oxygen with the wine, it can be helpful to leave the wine out in the decanter for thirty minutes to several hours before drinking. This additional time the wine spends "breathing" should coax out still more of its goodies for you to enjoy later.

The Bottom Line

Decanting for aeration is most beneficial for good quality young to middle-aged (less than eight years old) red wines and some superior quality, full-bodied white wines like good Chardonnay. However, decanting can quickly deplete older wines (more than eight years old) of their delicate aromas and flavors. Very old wines, in fact, often peak within ten to thirty minutes of opening just from sitting in your glass, making them ill fit for the shock of oxygen that comes with decanting for aeration.

"Sediment" in White Wines

Particles show up occasionally in white wines, particularly cool-climate white wines like those from chilly Germany and Switzerland. These crystal-like particles often look like shards of glass and, as you might imagine, can be a source of alarm to drinkers. Well, you can relax: These harmless crystals are just by-products of the tartaric acid that occurs naturally in all white wines. Nowadays most white wines go through a process called "cold stabilization" prior to release to ensure that these crystals don't form. But some traditionally made whites, especially those from Europe, still don't go through cold stabilization and wind up with—you got it—these harmless crystals in the bottle. And while you can certainly decant the wine to get them out, it's not necessary.

Decanting for Sediment

Older red wines, especially bigger-bodied reds like Barolo and Cabernet Sauvignon, often develop particles commonly referred to as sediment during the aging process. And while these particles are harmless, many people find it unsettling to see them floating in their glasses, especially if the wine is a rare and/or expensive one; in fact, many people will mistakenly decide that a wine with a little sediment is a flawed wine (it's not!). Besides this aesthetic consideration, sediment often tastes rather bitter and as a result it can take away from your enjoyment of a special bottle. For these reasons we often decant older reds to remove these undesirable particles. Here's how:

Step 1: Stand That Sucker Up!

If possible, stand an older red wine up a day or two before you plan to drink it in order to encourage all of its sediment to settle into the bottom. This is necessary because wine's normal storage position—on its side—assures that sediment gathers throughout the bottle over time.

Step 2: Pour in Front of a Bright Light

When you're ready to open it up, try to do so carefully, so you don't accidentally remix all the sediment into the wine (it should be at the bottom of the bottle at this point). The less movement the better here! Next, you'll want to decant the wine slowly and in one continuous pour, in front of a strong light source like a flashlight beam that will allow you to see the particles in the neck of the bottle just before they escape into the decanter. This will usually be about the time you've poured out nearly all of the wine, and this is when you should stop. The particles may be thick and chunky, like pencil shavings, or tiny and hazy, looking altogether like a dark cloud. No matter what, you don't want to drink it, so leave it in the bottle!

Step 3: Enjoy, and Be Quick About It

Now you're ready to pour the wine. Because older wines can quickly lose their gas, so to speak, it's best to pour the wine straightaway and drink it right up. Of course, this is the extreme case, for wines that are at their apex of maturity; and some wines with sediment are capable of lasting longer, for several hours or even more, after decanting. It totally depends. But if you're unsure of what you've got—a ten-minute wine or a three-hour wine—you might as well err on the side of caution. After all, there's nothing worse than cracking a really great bottle and then missing the show entirely.

> ## The Usual Suspects:
> ## Wines Requiring Decanting
>
> Some red wines develop particles over a period of just a few years in the bottle, but most don't begin

to really "throw" a heavy sediment, as is often said, until after eight to ten years. Besides Cabernet Sauvignon and Barolo, other frequent offenders include big reds that frequently show up in cellars, like Brunello di Montalcino, Super-Tuscans, Rhône reds, and some older red Burgundies. Vintage port is also famous for throwing some serious sediment, most often of the thick pencil shaving variety. If you're serving vintage port, I recommend first pouring it through a wine funnel or a coffee filter that's been rinsed with hot water to catch these giant particles.

Decanters and Their Stand-ins

A decanter is, essentially, a glorified carafe. A water pitcher with pizzazz, if you will. Decanters come in different sizes and styles, many of which have functional relevance and many of which do not. Generally, reach for simple, fairly narrow versions when decanting for sediment purposes and squatter decanters for your aeration needs. The best ones for aeration are those with giant bowls that afford wine the maximum possible surface-area exposure to oxygen. It's also worth noting that these big-bowled versions are the hardest to pour, so exercise caution. And, as you might imagine, when a true decanter's not handy, any sort of receptacle big enough to hold a bottle of wine will do the trick; as I mentioned before, I've even used flower vases as substitutes.

Party Time: Entertaining with Wine

While I understand that some of the most truly hip parties are those governed by the fewest rules, I think it's a good idea to at least have a good understanding of proper wine party etiquette. From there you can decide whether to throw what you've learned out the window and improvise or not—but at least you'll be a fabulously informed hip taster no matter what you do!

Setting the Scene

As I hope you'll recall from Chapter 2, there are some ideal conditions for wine tasting that you may want to put into play if you're hosting a more formal wine tasting, like one at which your guests will be actively paying attention to the wines' nuances, and possibly even taking notes. These ideal conditions include good lighting, a white background (remember that white napkins will do the trick), low noise, and an environment as free of strong odors as possible. You may also want to provide guests with notepaper and pens or pencils, if you're headed in the more formal wine-tasting direction.

Opening the Bottles

If you've got your foil cutter and corkscrew on hand, you're ready to start opening the wines you'll be serving. It's also helpful to have a towel or napkin on hand that can be used to wipe the inside of the bottle once the cork's been removed (older bottles have been known to leave behind some sediment, or even a little mold from older corks), and to wipe up the drips that may dribble down the bottle when you pour for your guests. Be sure to take a quick whiff of the wine to make sure it's not corked or flawed, and then serve away.

In terms of pouring, make sure you plan ahead so that each guest gets some wine. There are about twenty-four ounces of wine in a bottle, so if you have twelve guests and you'd like everyone to sample a certain bottle, plan on pouring about two ounces into each glass. This is roughly one third of a glass of wine. Also, avoid filling guests' glasses *too* full, since doing so doesn't allow room for swirling and may be overkill in terms of quantity.

Opening sparkling wines requires a little more TLC. Once you've removed the foil from the top of the bottle (you'll need to use your fingers or a small knife, since most foil cutters don't fit over Champagne bottles), be sure to keep a thumb on the cork while you remove the "cage." This is the wire enclosure that keeps the cork from spontaneously popping out at an inopportune time. And as you might guess, once you release some of the pressure holding the cork in place by removing the cage, the bottle's at risk of going "pop" before you're prepared. Be sure to keep the wine pointed *away* from yourself, any guests, and anything breakable, such as a light fixture, throughout the entire opening process. And, most critically, never, ever open a bottle while looking down at it; after all, losing an eye would be a terrible end to your party.

Once you've removed the cage, I recommend tossing a cloth or napkin over the bottle to catch the cork when it comes out. While pressing down on it continuously, twist the cork slowly until it comes out. When it does, you should hear a soft *ploof!* And although you'll miss out on the glorious *bang!* that accompanies shooting the cork out pell-mell as they do in the movies, you'll retain much more of the wine's bubble strength (some of which is lost during the movielike openings) and keep from inadvertently injuring any guests and/or breakables that might be nearby. Finally, pour away, preferably into flutes.

Storing Your Wine for Later

At any given time I'm likely to have as many as several, or even more—sometimes as many as six— open bottles of wine in my kitchen. This is partly because I frequently receive samples of new wines to try and can't possibly finish them in a single sitting (I know, you feel terrible for me), but also because I just love having lots of options on hand for meals and entertaining. I keep the open bottles fresh with simple, widely available Vacu Vin wine closures that remove much of the oxygen from open bottles by means of a vacuum pump system. This is an easy and inexpensive way to preserve wine for several days, or up to a week if it's kept in the fridge.

Gas methods are also gaining steam in the realm of at-home wine preservation. These work by forming a protective layer of inert gas between the surface of the wine and the oxygen in the bottle. Typically, gassed wines last about the same amount of time as those that have been vacuum sealed—from several days on up to a week. Whatever method you choose to use, investing in some of these tools will give you the freedom to enjoy a glass or two at a time without worrying about wasting the rest of the bottle. Being conservative was never so hip!

Order Matters

When serving two or more wines it's a good idea to take a moment to consider their relative weight, so that you can serve them in order of increasing intensity. The practical reason for this is that with wine, as with food, heavier versions overpower lighter renderings and make them seem flavorless and flat by comparison (in food, this is why you're best off serving a delicate soup before a chewy, reduction sauce–covered steak).

To that end, the tannin present to varying degrees in all red wines plays a big role in determining a wine's weight, and is largely responsible for why we almost always drink whites before reds in tasting scenarios. Generally speaking, dry sparkling wines and the most crisp, light-bodied white table wines should come first in a tasting, followed

by medium- and full-bodied whites, respectively, then reds. The same graduating rationale goes for the reds, with lighter wines like Pinot Noir coming before bigger reds like Syrah, Cabernet Sauvignon, and Zinfandel.

Sweet wines of any color pose a challenge to tasting line-ups, as they make dry wines tasted after them come across as bizarrely neutral at best and unappetizingly flat at worst. This is why any fully sweet wines should be served last in a tasting lineup (that means after the reds, even for fully sweet white wines), while those of mild to medium sweetness are best slotted in according to their weight. These in-betweener wines might include off-dry Champagnes and Kabinett- and Spätlese-level German Rieslings, whose light bodies necessitate placing them before bigger dry reds.

When to Mix It Up

As you might imagine, it's entirely possible to enjoy your wines even if you serve them *out* of this weight-guided order, and there are certainly occasions when mixing it up makes sense. A casual gathering in your home at which you'd rather not browbeat your guests into quaffing the good stuff in a particular order is a great example. It's not as though the wine police are going to show up at your door and demand that you cease and desist from tasting. At least, not on my watch.

How Much Wine Do I Need?

Depending on the nature and length of your party, you should plan on having anywhere from a half bottle to two thirds of a bottle of wine per guest. Although this may sound like a lot, it actually makes sense! To put this into perspective, consider that at a dinner party you may begin with a full glass of bubbly for each guest before pouring a different wine with each course. If you're serving several courses, that's four glasses of wine per person right there (a regular 750 ml bottle contains about six glasses of wine). And while there are certainly guests who won't consume this much of the good stuff, it's always better to have too much wine than too little.

Putting Together
a Dynamite Cheese Tray

Based on what you learned in Chapter 6, you've now got all the tools you need to put together a dynamite cheese tray for your party. The best cheese trays have an assortment of varying styles, usually a blue, a soft, a goat, and a semisoft cheese. Of course, there are tons of different cheeses that fall into these categories, and it can be fun to consult with a cheese merchant to find the most appropriate ones for your wines.

Besides an assortment of *fromage,* you might consider including some dried or fresh fruit, nuts, and possibly even some honey, preserves, or other sweet spreads like quince paste that complement cheeses' inherent saltiness. Last, make sure to put out plenty of bread or crackers and some knives, and you're good to go.

Quick Caveat on Booze Consumption by Your Guests

As a party-thrower, you have the responsibility to make sure your guests don't get so tanked they're not able to get home safely. Besides encouraging them to make use of designated drivers and taxis for transportation from your pad, putting out spittoons and plenty of water and making food available at all times are good ways to keep folks from getting excessively inebriated. Similarly, pacing your pours is important: If you'll be serving lots of wine throughout the evening, spacing it out over several hours will help your guests moderate their intake. 'Nough said.

Hip Wine-Tasting Party Ideas

There are lots of things you can do to up the hip quotient at your wine party. For starters, consider the ambience: Putting up a few decorations and using colorful paper to print out descriptions of the wines should pump things up significantly. Consider picking up wineglass name tags or charms to put around the stems of the glasses; these have the dual benefits of making things seem more festive while helping guests keep track of their stems, and are widely available online or through specialty wine retailers like Beverages & More. You can also use offbeat "spittoons" such as flower vases and punch bowls to lend a sense of whimsy to the event.

And finally, never underestimate the impact of wine and food pairings. I've found that party guests *love* sampling specially prepared wine and food pairings such as crab cakes with Sauvignon Blanc and stuffed mushrooms with Pinot Noir. Taking the extra time to prepare (even if that means buying them premade!) and set out specific foods that pair with the wines you're pouring can go a long way in upping the "*ooh*" factor at your party.

Time to Shop

Savvy revelers know that every great house party starts with a shopping trip. And whether you're buying wine for your gathering, for yourself, or for a gift, the next chapter contains useful tips on navigating wine retailers of all kinds and making sense of their wares. And so with no further ado, *let's go shopping!*

Gucci Wine at a Target Price

Since I'm someone who's lived in Paris, spent countless hours poring over fashion magazines, and even written about *la mode,* it probably comes as little surprise that one of my favorite things to do is partake of a sample sale. Considered the Holy Grail for the fashion bargain hunter, sample sales are warehouse sales in which designer duds are offered at rock-bottom prices.

So when I met a wine merchant who compared his philosophy on selling wine to the fashion world's sample sales, I knew this was someone I could relate to. His process involves buying excess high-end wine at a discount and reblending it, then selling it under his own label at prices far below what the stuff would've sold for under its intended brand. He calls his concept "Gucci wine at a Target price," and I think it's brilliant.

Happily, there are lots of enlightened wine merchants like my friend marketing their wines in innovative ways, whether it's via a creative analogy like fashion or helpful in-store tools. These merchants include retailers that group wines according to easy-to-understand categories like recommended food pairings (e.g., "seafood wines"), the weight of wines (e.g., "light and crisp") or wines' flavor profiles. Also, some wine bars have begun to sell wine by the bottle, so curious customers can sample before buying, and specialty stores have started furnishing wine information kiosks, tasting notes, and other DIY shopping tools. Besides all this, there's a whole bevy of innovative online merchants offering forward-thinking tools to help you find the perfect bottle. Read on for tips on navigating the fashionably diverse world of wine shopping.

Chapter 9

Shop Till You Drop

So Many Options

Now that you're well versed in the ins and outs of the good stuff, it's time to put your budding knowledge to work, and to venture out into the world of wine retailing. And what a wide and varied world it is! The retail wine landscape essentially breaks down into four major types of sellers: specialty wine shops; warehouse stores; online retailers; and, in many states, supermarkets. In this chapter I'll address each one of them and outline strategies for you to find the best bottles in their midst, pointing out along the way common retail pitfalls and how to avoid them.

Specialty Wine Shops

My favorite wine retailers, specialty shops of all sizes are where you have the greatest likelihood of meeting passionate salespeople who not only know what they're talking about but are also genuinely interested in helping you.

The Little Guys

At first glance the best small specialty wine shops look no different from your average neighborhood store: They're usually tucked into a side street under an unassuming facade, and might have a few of their finest wares displayed in the window. Venture inside these homey spots and you're likely to find friendly salespeople and possibly even the owner him- or herself waiting to help you make a choice based on tonight's dinner, a special occasion, or whatever else brought you into the shop. You might call these stores the vinous equivalent of a small clothing boutique: The products are usually limited but well chosen, and the service can be excellent.

But, as is the case with any specialty retailer, it's also easy to feel pressured by the attention from the sales staff in these small shops. When you walk in, it's polite to say hello to the employee or owner of the establishment, but don't hesitate to then say that you'd just like to take a moment to look around when you're asked if you'd like assistance. Personally, I like to get the lay of the store, so to speak, before I launch into a conversation with any retail clerk. This has nothing to do with an inherent distrust of these folks; instead, I just like to take a moment to look around and size up the selection, check out the way the wine is organized, and inspect the condition of the bottles.

Bigger Specialty Shops

The main difference between small specialty wine shops and their bigger brethren is selection. Larger shops can be of the independent-retailer-around-the-corner variety (like the little guys) or parts of larger chains, but either way they'll usually carry more wines from more places, and have a larger staff to go along with it. At my favorite bigger wine specialty retailer, K&L Wine Merchants in San Francisco and Los Angeles, members of the staff specialize in different regions of the wine world, so there's usually someone on hand who can answer questions about the *premiers crus* of Burgundy, someone else who can recommend a great Rioja Reserva, and still a different gal who'll give you the lowdown on the best small-production Champagnes they carry.

This sort of depth of expertise is ideal, although hardly normal. At the other end of the expertise spectrum when it comes to these bigger shops—especially at the chains— you can be hard-pressed to find a clerk who knows the difference between Ketel One and Opus One. It totally varies. My advice is to seek out the better bigger merchants like K&L and shop there whenever you can. Finding them will take some trial and error, so don't hesitate to shop around until you feel like you've found a good fit. To give you a hand, I've included a list in the Appendix of some of my favorite bigger wine merchants.

The Bottom Line

No matter what its size, a great specialty wine shop contains a knowledgeable, friendly staff, and interesting wine kept in good conditions.

Top Wines for $10 and Under

Reach for These Wallet-Friendly Wines When You Don't Want to Break the Bank (Prices May Vary Slightly)

Sparkling

Domaine Ste. Michelle Blanc de Blancs, Columbia Valley, Washington
Segura Viudas Brut Reserva Cava, Spain

Whites

Baron Philippe de Rothschild Chardonnay, Vin
de Pays d'Oc, France
Loosen Bros. "Dr. L" Riesling, Mosel, Germany
Marqués de Riscal Rueda, Spain
Pine Crest Chenin Blanc Coastal Region, South
Africa
Veramonte Sauvignon Blanc Casablanca Valley
Reserva, Chile

Rosés

Bon-Bon Shiraz Rosé, South Australia
Goats do Roam Rosé, Coastal Region, South
Africa
Les Jamelles Cinsault Rosé, Vin de Pays d'Oc,
France
Marqués de Cáceres Rosado, Rioja, Spain
Toad Hollow Eye of the Toad Pinot Noir Rosé,
Sonoma, California

Reds

Banrock Station Shiraz, South Eastern Australia
Bodegas Catena Zapata Cabernet Sauvignon,
Mendoza Alamos, Argentina
Bogle Vineyards Merlot, California
Columbia Crest "Two Vines" Cabernet
Sauvignon, Columbia Valley, Washington
Pepperwood Grove Pinot Noir, California

Assessing a Shop's Storage MO

You'll probably recall that a bottle stored on its side keeps
the wine in contact with its cork, ensuring it stays moist

and plump and the wine safe from the damaging effects of excessive oxygenation. This is why wine shops that keep bottles on hand for any longer than a few weeks should keep them stored on their sides. These bottles might include old and rare wines that may sit in the store for months or even years before being sold. For wines that are likely to sell in the near future, this is less of a concern. (In fact, many shops display wines expected to sell quickly in an upright position in order to save space—and there's nothing wrong with this.)

Besides having conscientious bottle storage, the shop shouldn't be too hot. Because we know that wine does poorly at warm temperatures for any period of time, shops that seem hot are at serious risk of containing bad bottles, and should be avoided. Other red flags that might warn you to shop elsewhere include old, excessively faded, or torn labels, which indicate that the wine is in all likelihood in poor condition *or* has been there for an eternity—neither a good sign! Bottles with thick layers of dust are not only scary to look at but definitely a sign that the inventory isn't turning over much around those parts—also a bad sign. Move on.

I'll Take My Wine with a Parka, Please

Some innovative retailers take wine storage so seriously that they've started keeping their stores at cellar temperature. One New Jersey retailer has even gone so far as to call itself 56 Degree Wine, and Moore Brothers in New York has started giving out parkas to customers when they walk in. Visiting these spots makes for a chilly but rewarding experience, as you can be absolutely certain that each and every bottle is stored at precisely the right temperature.

Asking for Help

Assuming the shop's wines seem to be in good condition, you'll either want to make a selection on your own or ask for help. If you'd like help from the shop's owner or a clerk, then now's the time to ask for it, clearly and confidently. The same logic applies to asking for help in a retail wine shop as in a restaurant: You might consider telling the clerk what kind of food you'll be having with the wine, that you prefer a "rich, robust red" (or similar stylistic description), or that you'd like to spend ten dollars, and not a penny more. All of these criteria, or a combination thereof, are totally acceptable and will help you home in on a bottle that suits your needs and budget.

Of course, there's always the inevitable gamble that comes with trying something new—meaning, the bottle you wind up with might not be the wine of your dreams, no matter how clearly you state your case or how savvy the clerk. But the good news is that by taking a chance and trying something new, you've just gotten one step closer to finding a wine you like. Now *that's* something to get excited about.

Label-Reading Essentials

How to decode those pesky labels

No doubt about it, a visit to the wine store can be a daunting task with all the languages, critters, colors, and jargon that show up on labels these days. Follow these rules of thumb to help sift through the confusion:

• Determine if the wine is named for a place or a grape (see Chapter 1). This is your best bet for figuring out what's in the bottle. Based on what you now know about wines made in places that tend to use place-based naming (e.g., France, Spain, Italy, Germany), determining where a wine comes from gives you vital clues as to its contents. Italy's Barolo, for example, will be made from a single grape, Nebbiolo. Use what you know about the Nebbiolo grape, recent Italian vintages, and your own personal tastes to go from there.

- If the wine is named for something *besides* a grape or a place (e.g., 2005 Opus One Napa Valley), you'll have to work harder. For example, you may recall from Chapter 4 that Opus One is what's called a Meritage wine, a wine made in the Bordeaux style in the United States. In this case you can safely assume that it's a blend of two or more of the following grapes: Cabernet Sauvignon, Merlot, Cabernet Franc, Petit Verdot, and Malbec.
- German labels are among the trickiest to decipher, but they give you a hand in that they often state the name of the grape used as well (e.g., 2005 Dr. Loosen Ürziger Würzgarten Riesling, Mosel-Saar-Ruwer).
- Never pick a wine just because it has a cute label. Although I fully support creativity when it comes to label art, this should be the last thing that you consider when making your choice. Instead, think about the occasion you're buying for, your budget, your food pairing (if applicable), and your own tastes. If a wine satisfies all of these criteria *and* looks cute, then so much the better.
- Don't hesitate to ask for help! Remember the tips outlined in this chapter to determine if your shop's clerk is dispensing good knowl-

edge, and if so, get started on getting the help you need to land a great bottle. After all, good clerks in reputable establishments *want* to help you find exactly what you need!

More Than Just a Wine Store

Besides the benefit of personalized service, some of the better specialty wine merchants also offer wine classes and tastings that are great ways for budding oenophiles like yourself to expand your knowledge of wine. Plus, classes can make a store feel sort of like a community center for wine—your local contact point with the wine world, you might say. Frequently held in a special room or section of the store on weekends or weekday evenings, wine classes and tastings invariably feature wines for sale in the stores, which means that if you really like something you try in your class, you're in the perfect place to pick some up. Plus, who *wouldn't* want to drink some great wine at 2:00 P.M. on a Saturday!?

Quick Tip. Next time you're in your local wine shop, inquire if the place offers classes or tastings; if it does, grab a schedule and try to fit one in. For a listing of local wine events—including classes—in communities across the country, visit localwineevents.com.

Sizing Up the Smarts of the Staff

Specialty wine merchants both big and small are where you're likely to find the most knowledge-able staff. But, as with anything in life, expertise when it comes to wine sales is a mixed bag. The ideal scenario is a shop in which a member of the staff offers help readily when asked and can speak knowledgeably about key wine topics and the store's inventory. To quickly size up the smarts of a clerk in any retail wine shop, consider asking him or her the following questions:

- What's the difference between a *premier cru* and a *grand cru* Burgundy? (They're both high-end Pinot Noirs from France's Burgundy region, and *grand crus* are the best you can buy, therefore better than *premier crus*.)
- What kind of wine is a Super-Tuscan? (The key here is that it's a wine from traditionally Sangiovese-centric Tuscany made in the so-called international style and often includes non-Italian varieties like Cabernet Sauvignon or Merlot with traditionally Italian Sangiovese.)
- How does New Zealand Sauvignon Blanc differ from Sancerre? (Sancerre is Sauvignon Blanc from France's Loire Valley and considered to be more mellow and mineral-laced than assertive New Zealand Sauvignons.)

If a clerk has trouble answering any of these questions, there's probably a better place out yonder for your wine shopping.

Hip to Know: Avoid Clearance Wines

This isn't a used-car lot or a stereo sale, so be wary of wines that have been excessively marked down, those that are on clearance, or anything of the sort.

These may be wines for which a retailer received a "deal" from a distributor (for possibly dubious reasons) or on which he or she is making a significant markup. Neither of these scenarios is a good reason for you to make an impulse buy, so don't. Occasionally, however, merchants will mark down a wine in order to move it out of their inventory before the next vintage of the same wine arrives. These are the only instances in which I recommend buying wines that have been significantly marked down, provided you can assess that this is the rationale behind the reduction (don't hesitate to ask). If you're unsure, wait for the new vintage; it'll be there before you know it.

Warehouse Stores: Bring On the Big Box!

Costco, it turns out, is the number one wine retailer in the United States. That's right: numero uno, the big dog, with upward of $600 million in annual wine sales. The best reason to buy wine at warehouse retailers like Costco is that their prices are often outstanding, thanks to the deep discounts these retailers negotiate with their significant buying power. But there's a downside to these discounts: Inventory can be spotty (because it's mostly based on what's available to them at discount) and you may not find the same wines there twice, for the same reason. So, if you decide to shop at these spots you should count on taking a hit when it comes to selection and consistency compared to most other wine retailers.

Another drawback to shopping at warehouse stores is that they rarely have wine-educated staff on hand to help you out. If you're lucky, there'll be a single staffer there to answer wine-related questions, but it can often be tough to track this person down. When you do, you may have to wait as he or she assists the swarms of other customers who are inevitable at these kinds of places. And finally, the stores can be short on self-help tools such as "shelf-talkers"—essentially tasting notes posted near wines for wine shoppers—meaning that unless you're already familiar with many of the brands there, it can be downright frustrating to try to figure out what to buy.

Thinking *Inside* the Box

Time was, swilling boxed wine was the vinous equivalent of shopping for clothes at Target: It just wasn't done. But, just as Target has started selling clothes you might actually consider wearing, so too have boxed wines dramatically upped their consumer appeal. Taking a cue from growing demand for wine in so-called alternative packaging, perfectly respectable wineries have started producing boxed wine, often with juice they would otherwise sell in regular 750 ml bottles. Better yet, many of today's boxes include collapsible pouches inside that keep wine safe from the harmful effects of oxidation for up to several weeks, or even a month, in your fridge. Practical, too!

Among the better boxes are northern California's Black Box, the Delicato Bota Box, Banrock Station's boxes, and those from Hardys Stamp of Australia. Even Target's gotten in on the act, peddling the undeniably cute Target Wine Cube in its stores!

Warehouse Shopping: How to Deal

So, how do you make the best of the situation? First, you'll need to do a little more legwork when it comes to researching the wines available at big box retailers. Some warehouse stores have Web sites with frequently updated product listings, and this is a great way to check out the inventory before you go.

Try thinking of warehouse wine shopping as a complement to your regular wine shopping, and don't be frustrated if you can't score everything you need there. Costco, for example, tends to carry lots of high-end Bordeaux reds and vintage ports, as well as multipacks of the same kinds of wine (great for gifts). So if you're looking to put together a mixed case of inexpensive whites, rosés, and reds from around the world, this probably isn't the best place. The sooner you get used to that, the better off you'll be.

Small Was Never So Good

Besides appearing in better boxed versions, wine is showing up more and more in another kind of alternative packaging: the single serving. Whether these come in minisized glass or plastic bottles or the faddish new recyclable Tetra Paks (hilariously similar to the juice boxes we used to quaff from as kids), single servings make a lot of sense for folks who're looking to take wine where glass can't go, like on picnics or to the beach. They're perfect for people who just don't want to crack a whole bottle, and I just love the flexibility and informality of the size.

My favorites are the colorful, juice box–esque single-serving packs from California's Three Thieves, which makes a Merlot, a Cab, and a Pinot Grigio, among others. Watch for more and more single servings on shelves in the near future— they're the next big (er, small) thing in wine.

Location, Location, Location

If you live in a big city like LA, San Francisco, Chicago, or New York, consider yourself very, *very* lucky when it comes to wine shopping. For everyone else, you're going to have to work harder, in some instances *much* harder, to find a good wine store in your area. If you find yourself in the unlucky situation of residing somewhere without a good wine merchant nearby, consider taking the occasional trip to a nearby town or city where there *is* one. In these instances you can make it worth your while by stocking up on a case or two to enjoy over the following weeks before trekking back. Better yet: Many stores will ship or deliver wine to you (especially when this doesn't require shipping across state lines), which means you can opt to phone in your order next time.

Fortunately, the rise in great Web sites selling unique wines from around the country and the world means that many of you can now go online to shop, although some archaic laws prohibiting the shipping of wine to customers in certain states mean this still isn't possible for everyone. (These laws, unfortunately, are holdovers from our Prohibition days and completely outdated!) Assuming you live in a state where wineries *can* ship to you,★ becoming a member of a by-the-month wine club or two will ensure that you receive some of the good stuff on a regular basis, without the hassle of traveling for it. Check out the section "Wine Club Know-How" in this chapter for advice on choosing a club that fits your needs and budget.

Shopping Online: The New Frontier

There's no better place to shop for wine these days than on the Internet—assuming you can receive wine shipments where you live. In 2005 the United States Supreme Court

★ For a current list of states accepting cross-border wine shipments, visit wineinstitute.org.

made a landmark decision overturning archaic laws that prohibited folks in more than twenty states from receiving wine shipments from outside their borders. Unfortunately, many states remain mired in their own internal battles in the aftermath of the Court's ruling (which said that states can ultimately decide themselves whether or not to accept shipments), preventing their good citizens from enjoying the fruits of the high court's decision. If you live in one of the currently ineligible states, my sincerest condolences go out to you, as do my hopes that the situation reverses itself as soon as possible.

On the upside, this whole rigmarole has led a bevy of speculative wine e-tailers to throw their hats into the ring and start up innovative businesses, with plans to sell wine online to newly eligible customers. Many of these sites offer creative online tools and helpful content aimed at assisting folks like you in making informed online wine-shopping decisions. Even better, many of the sites specialize in certain kinds of wine (e.g., only Austrian wines, or exclusively boutique or small-production wines), allowing you to browse extensive selections of very specific wines, all from the comfort of your own home. Check out the list of my favorite wine e-tailers in the Appendix.

Top Spots for Wine Online

bottlenotes.com
>   Wine clubs tailored to your personal taste profile.

klwines.com
>   Great product info, real-time inventory count.

sherry-lehmann.com
>   Extensive selection, great customer service.

winebid.com
  Most extensive Internet-based wine auction
  site.
winemonger.com
  Extensive online selection of Austrian wine.
wine-searcher.com
  Searchable database of over eight thousand
  wine merchants; find prices and locations of
  specific wines across the United States.
zachys.com
  Top New York–based e-tailer and auction
  house.

Wine Shipping Don'ts

- Don't have wine shipped to you in the middle of summer or the dead of winter if you can avoid it. Heat is particularly damaging to wine, and unless a retailer has assured you that your wine will be shipped in a refrigerated container, skip it. Excessive cold also isn't good for wine, so if you're receiving a shipment in winter, make sure someone is available to receive your shipment and bring it indoors.
- Don't have wine sent to a place where an adult isn't available to sign for it. Packages containing alcoholic beverages require the signature of an adult over the age of twenty-one.
- Don't have your wine sent someplace where it might be stolen while waiting for you to pick it up. Wine shipments, which often state that they require an adult signature (implying that they contain alcohol), are among the most frequently stolen packages.

Drumroll, Please:
Buying Wine in the Supermarket

Without a doubt, I get more questions from folks asking how they can make a safe choice when buying wine in the supermarket than any other wine shopping–related question. Which makes sense, if you think about it: As Americans, we do the lion's share of our grocery shopping at these food emporiums, and their wine selections tend to be boring at best and utterly bereft of decent choices at worst. And although not all states allow wine sales at supermarkets, they're one of this land's highest-volume wine sales channels. No wonder so many people call me from the aisles of supermarkets begging for a tip or two on how to pick up a bottle that won't bear a disturbing resemblance to Welch's grape juice!

We can thank these gargantuan stores' complex distribution networks for their frustratingly limited selections: In order to gain a slot on the shelves of most large supermarkets, a winery must not only produce enough to make it worth the stores' while, but it's also got to get on board with a distributor who'll sell its wares to the stores in the first place (in the United States we have a three-tiered distribution system for alcohol that requires wineries to first sell their wares to licensed distributors or wholesalers, who then sell the wine to retailers).

Together, these factors can be a prohibitively tall order for, say, a small winery in Oregon producing just a few hundred cases of little-known Pinot Noir. So, instead of selecting one of its interesting Oregonian Pinots, you get to choose between one or two generic big-brand Pinots in your supermarket wine aisle, assuming the store is enlightened enough to carry Pinot in the first place.

Supermarket Safe Bets

Because supermarkets aren't going to stop being a major part of our lives anytime soon, I offer the following tips for tracking down decent bottles in even the grimmest supermarket wine aisles.

- **Reach for the *riserva*.**

    Chianti Riserva, that is. For some reason, most super-markets carry at least one Chianti or a few different ones. But as you'll hopefully recall, Chianti is of widely varying quality, so try to find versions labeled *riserva* or *classico riserva* (the best) to be safe.

- **Spring for bubbles.**

    Widely available in supermarkets, since many people buy bubbles on special occasions like New Year's, non-vintage Champagne from a good producer is always a safe bet.

- **Make it a Cava night.**

    For the same reason as Champagne, Spanish Cava is widely available in grocery stores. Snap up these tradi-tional method sparklers when you're looking to spend less than you would on Champagne. Freixenet is a pretty good one, and widely available.

- **Say good-bye to the oak.**

    Unoaked whites are your new best friends when it comes to the supermarket wine aisle. Because the worst wines at supermarkets pander to the oak chip-oblivious masses, reach for crisp unoaked whites like New Zealand Sauvignon Blanc whenever possible.

- **Find a few friends and stick by them.**

    Perhaps this goes without saying, but your best strategy for buying decent wine in the supermarket is to find a few bottles you find palatable and keep buying them. Perhaps the only upside to grocery store wine shopping is consistency: This is the one place you can count on finding the same stuff over and over again.

Wine Club Know-How

Wine club memberships are great ways to ensure that you receive regular shipments of wines from some of your fa-vorite wineries. By the same logic, they're also great if you live in an area without a stellar wine merchant nearby!

A wine club works like a subscription service: Once you

sign up, a winery sends you shipments of wine periodically, in previously agreed-upon quantities. For example, you might sign up to receive two bottles a month, one bottle a quarter, or a case every other month. Club memberships also are great ways to receive a favorite producer's limited production and library wines (often not available to non–club members). Given the growing ease of shipping wine to customers, lots of retailers now offer wine clubs as well, and their clubs are often based on themes (e.g., the Red Wine Only Club, the Champagne Club, the Spanish Wine Club). The number of choices and flexibility vary by retailer, so make sure you get all the details before signing up.

The best wine clubs are those that give members a heads-up as to what they can expect to receive in their next shipment, and offer folks the opportunity to decline receiving it, or to receive just a part of the shipment (e.g., you can elect to receive the red but not the white wine they're planning to send). This element of choice has evolved in part out of the unfortunate habit of some wineries using wine club shipments—for which members prepay or are billed automatically on their credit cards—to unload difficult-to-sell or undesirable bottles. Happily, visionary wineries understand that wine clubs are wonderful ways to build their brands—as their members become brand emissaries, quite literally—and never send subpar bottles.

Due to many wineries' small production levels, some of the best wine clubs are incredibly tough to get into and have long waiting lists of folks hankering to get on board. And because some wineries sell *only* to their club members, this scarcity is another great reason to sign up. If you visit a small winery, really love its products, and believe it's going to "take off" before long, signing up for its club will ensure that you can continue to enjoy its wines even when they become hard to find. To learn about clubs, visit the Web sites of some of your favorite wineries, which usually have a page dedicated to outlining the perks and prices associated with their clubs.

Wine Ratings: The Lowdown

Wine ratings are a contentious subject, and for a great reason: Wine, like art and music, is a subjective thing. In other words, while I may love the music of one band, you may be quite certain that its music isn't fit to play for a pack of howling dogs. Same band, completely different takes on its quality.

The same goes for wine, which is why folks often get up in arms when any one particular critic of the stuff is awarded what they believe to be excessive influence over consumers' opinions and buying patterns. But I think that wine ratings, when taken with a grain of salt, can actually be quite helpful in deciding which wine you'd like to buy, particularly if you're looking for an outside opinion before purchasing a bottle for a special occasion.

Three of the most influential sources of wine criticism are Robert Parker, Stephen Tanzer, and *Wine Spectator* magazine. I happen to think they're all credible, although I shy away from relying too heavily on any one of them. Instead, my strategy is to perk up and pay attention to their ratings when *more than one of them* weighs in positively on a wine. These are the lucky occasions when you can rule out a good deal of the subjectivity involved, and feel confident their assessments are pretty accurate.

All three of these sources operate subscription-based Web sites where you can pay for access to their ratings and commentary (they are erobert parker.com, wineaccess.com, and winespectator .com, respectively). If you'd rather not subscribe, conducting a Google search on a wine you're interested in learning more about will often yield abridged versions of critics' notes as well as additonal commentary from bloggers, e-zines, and retailers.

Returns and How-To

If a wine you've purchased is corked, or just tastes off (re-member the list of flaws and their descriptions from Chap-ter 2?), recork it and return it, with the receipt, as soon as possible. For obvious reasons a merchant won't look fondly on bottles returned two-thirds empty. In fact, I'll often pour the offending glass or glasses back into the bottle just to show the merchant that I'm not trying to dupe him or her. In the case that the wine simply doesn't suit your fancy, you have a tougher job ahead of you in convincing the merchant to take the bottle back, because this is really a matter of subjective taste. But if you believe the merchant made a poor recommendation based on information you gave him or her, you may have a case. The power of persua-sion rests in your hands here.

The return process is easiest at specialty wine merchants, who will almost always take back flawed bottles with few or no questions; at bigger merchants that don't specialize in wine, on the other hand, such as warehouse stores and su-permarkets, the task is tougher, and return policies will vary by store. To save yourself a trip, consider calling ahead and asking to speak to a manager to see if they accept wine returns.

For Old and Rare Wines, Go the Extra Mile

The nature of retailers in the United States (and in most parts of the world, for that matter) is to sell wines when they're shipped to stores, whether the stuff is at its ideal, or peak, drinking time or not. And because most wineries have an understandable desire to move their product out the door as soon as possible—as opposed to incurring the hefty costs related to storing it for years and years—it's generally the case that many wines that are meant to be drunk down the road wind up on our retail shelves much too early, before their ideal drinking time. Wines that fall into this category include Bordeaux reds, vintage ports, some Napa Cabs, and Barolos, among others.

A few of the better merchants—usually of the specialty merchant variety—*will* actually keep some older wines on hand, often in a special "old and rare" section of their stores. But these merchants are the exception rather than the rule, especially as American consumption skews increasingly toward the habit of buying wine to consume the same night rather than to lay down in a cellar for a far-off day.

Auctions Explained

So, what to do if you'd like to pick up some older wine that's perfectly primed for drinking today? Your best bet is to head to an auction. Auctions are *the* place to track down old and rare wines that are drinking well now, although you'll need to exercise caution to make sure you wind up with product *of good provenance*, as they like to say. Wines of good provenance are those that previously belonged to honest folks who took good care of the bottles—most important, keeping them in tip-top storage conditions. Auction houses do the best they can to source wines from this kind of seller, and when they're sure the bottles come from a reliable source—from good provenance—they'll reflect this fact in the price.

The best-known auction houses are Sotheby's and Christie's, although a growing number of savvy online auctioneers are making it easier than ever to bid for wine, and often at lower prices than their tony counterparts. WineBid.com, for example, offers not only old and rare wines but also a good assortment of single bottles and odd lots of wines of varying quality and price levels. If you're looking to dabble in wine auctions for the first time, this is a great place to start.

Wine Futures

Another way to secure rare wines is to buy them as wine futures, a process sometimes referred to by the French term *en primeur*. *En primeur* sales occur before a wine is bottled, when it's still in the cask, and therefore long before the wine is actually delivered. A fairly recent phenomenon, future sales are sometimes viewed as investments due to the long lead time (sometimes as much as two years before the wines are delivered) that buyers must wait before they can actually pop the cork on these wines.

Wines sold as futures are mostly in-demand wines meant for the cellar, such as top Bordeaux and Cabernet Sauvignon–based reds from the likes of Napa Valley. The idea behind futures it that by paying for them up front, consumers secure these rare wines and pay less than the market will command for them down the line. But this is not always the case, which is why futures are also risky.

Bon Voyage

Now that you're up to speed on the major grape varieties of the world, tasting wine, pairing it with food, shopping, and entertaining with the stuff, what more could you need to know? Why, the best part of all—traveling for wine! Read on for the final chapter in your *Hip Tastes* journey, in which you'll find tips for planning and making the most of your wine travels, wherever they may take you.

Oh, How Far You'll Go!

When I was twenty I spent an unforgettable semester living in Paris. There were so many things I loved about that city: fabulous shopping, amazing nightlife, unbeatable culture, and fantastic dining were just a few of them. But just as exciting to me was the opportunity that living in Paris afforded to explore France's famous wine regions during my time off from school: Many weekends found me catching trains to hallowed wine spots like Burgundy and Champagne while my friends set off for wild week-ends in the likes of Amsterdam and Munich. Same level of enthusiasm, different priorities.

Years later my enthusiasm for wine-country travel has only grown. I've returned to France on several occasions since then, on each visit venturing back into the vineyards to learn more about the people who tend the vines and make the good stuff we enjoy so much. I'm also a frequent traveler to California's many storied wine regions, areas I consider myself extremely lucky to have almost literally in my backyard. My travels both near and far have shown me that there's something wonderful and a little magical about visiting the places where wine is made; seeing where it all goes down makes it come to life in a fabulous new light.

Chapter 10

Wine Country Travel

All Aboard!

As your interest in the good stuff grows, taking a trip to check out the vineyards, personalities, and regions that make great wine will allow you to build upon your appreciation and passion for it. You might say it's like consummating your wine relationship—it'll take you and the good stuff to a whole new level of intimacy. And so with no further ado, read on for wine country travel tips and advice that'll have you on the road to enjoying wine on its own turf in no time.

Planning Your Trip

If you're lucky enough to live in places with thriving wine industries like California and New York State, it can be easy to fit in a little wine country travel on the weekends. For others, visiting wine country requires a little more effort and planning. No matter what, you'll be rewarded for your efforts with warm hospitality, lifelong memories, and a better understanding of wine, so it's well worth your while! And did I mention that wine country is one of the most romantic places to take your sweetie? It also makes a dynamite destination for group celebrations like bachelor and bachelorette parties, or any other fun event that gives you an excuse to go.

A Few Considerations

As with most things in life, the more you put into planning your trip, the more you're likely to get out of it. This is why it's a great idea to do some homework before you go to wine country, including asking yourself and your companions a few key questions to make sure you're on the same page in terms of what you're looking to get out of your travels. Here are a few good things to ask before you go:

- Is wine tasting our main goal while there, or are we also interested in doing other things (e.g., sightseeing, visiting relatives, shopping, etc.)?
- Are we interested in dining and nightlife too, or would we rather be somewhere secluded and remote with fewer diversions but more privacy?
- Do we want to chart our own course, or might we want to hire a guide to take care of all the details?
- And finally, the all-important inquiry: *How big a concern is our budget?* (Note: Read on for some great tips on wine country travel on the cheap!)

Day Tripping

Who says going to wine country has to be a serious commitment? If you live close to wine country you can get a taste of the experience without staying over—which means you can save money *and* get back home in time to go to that party, catch a flick, or do whatever else pleases you on a Saturday night. In some cities with wine country close by, you can even catch a bus or coach at a central location in the morning that will deposit you back at the same spot that night, making it more or less effortless to fit a little wine country into your weekend. Plus, you don't have to worry about driving—which is always nice when tasting!

Going with a Group

These may seem like pretty straightforward considerations, but I think you'd be surprised at how often travelers have very different ideas of what a wine country visit has in store for them. Some folks are content to visit just a winery or two during their stay, choosing instead to spend much of their time on long meals, exploring the countryside or other tourist attractions nearby, or even hanging around a spa or resort. If you have high hopes for fitting in as many winery tours as possible and find long meals a waste of time, on the other hand, it's probably a good idea to air those thoughts to your fellow travelers prior to departure! This way you can plan your itinerary accordingly (and manage your gang's expectations).

When Nightlife's on the Agenda

These considerations will also affect where you decide to go on your trip. If you're interested in tapping into some local dining and nightlife while in wine country, I'd recommend steering clear of really rural areas like northern California's Mendocino County, which is known for its delicious cool climate wines but most definitely not for its nightlife. Ditto for France's famous Burgundy, although if you're savvy you can find a handful of fantastic restaurants tucked into the small towns there. California's Sonoma and Napa counties, on the other hand, contain a bevy of interesting restaurants, and even a few good lounges and bars that cater to those areas' thriving tourist trades and the appetites of adventurous locals. These make ideal destinations for wine country travelers looking to soak in some ambience outside the vineyards and tasting rooms.

Get the Lowdown Online

To find out more about the diversions available in areas you're considering for your trip, I recommend consulting wine travel resources online, such as winecountry.com. You can often size up an area's potential by checking how many restaurant, shopping, and resort listings there are for it on such sites. Wine travel blogs are also great resources for first-person accounts of places to go and things to do in wine country. You can find lots of these with a simple Google search, but expect some serious variation in terms of quality and breadth of content.

Charting Your Own Course Versus Hiring a Guide

Generally, I prefer to chart my own course in wine country, but there are times when, logistically speaking, it can make a lot of sense to go with a guided tour. This can be a good idea when traveling abroad, where you may not be familiar with the language, driving rules and conditions, local customs, and other key inputs into your travel equation. It might also make sense when you're just limited on time and can't put together your own itinerary before heading out.

If you do decide to go with a guide, it can be fun to seek out tours that put an adventurous and sometimes hands-on twist on the traditional tour. These might include bike tours, vineyard "treks," and balloon rides as well as indoor activities like wine-blending exercises, cooking classes, and wine-tasting boot camps. I think you'll find with a little research that the most-visited wine regions in the world offer a ton of unique experiences like this, and they can really add to the impact of your trip. And after all, you've got the rest of your life to just sit on the wine train and soak it all in; for now, in can be terrifically fun to get active and hands-on in wine country!

Finding a Guide

There are literally thousands of wine country touring and guide companies located throughout the world, and they vary widely in terms of offerings and quality. Besides an Internet search, one thing you can do to sift through all the options is consult with a concierge or helpful staffer at your hotel, if you've already decided where you're going to stay, or with the local tourist bureau there. The latter in particular can be terrifically helpful in recommending reliable tours and guides based on your needs.

On a recent trip to Bordeaux I was delighted to find at the Bordeaux office of tourism a wealth of information about local wineries and activities, and the spot's helpful staff even set up several tasting appointments for my companion and me. Their help proved indispensable in that vast and sometimes confusing region!

Parlez-Vous My Language?

When traveling abroad it's a good idea to inquire with guide companies and tourism offices about tours led in English. Particularly in countries like France, where many wine country tourists are natives, winery tours are often led in that country's language. Special tours in English are usually offered as well, but they're often scheduled at specific times, and sometimes only on certain days of the week. Your guide will probably have accounted for this, but if you're charting your own course it's definitely worth checking with a tourism office or with the wineries themselves as to the language you can expect to hear on your visits. After all, a tour in French in France may *sound* romantic, but what's much better is actually understanding it!

Charting Your Own Course

Particularly for wine country visits stateside, it can be a lot of fun and logistically realistic to plan your own trip. This often makes the most sense for shorter trips like weekend getaways, during which you'll probably visit several wineries, have a nice meal or two, and enjoy some rest and relaxation in a cozy B&B or similar wine country retreat. Unburdened by language and custom barriers, you'll be able to make your own reservations and arrangements without the aid of a tourism office, hotel concierge, or travel agent. But keep in mind that these same resources can still be quite helpful in assisting you with things like scoring reservations at off-the-beaten-path wineries, tough-to-get-into restaurants, and the like. So, don't dis the local wine country tourist bureau★ just because you're stateside!

How Many Wineries Is Too Many?

I find that visiting a winery before lunch and two or three afterward is just about right when it comes to wine-tasting visits. If you've called ahead for a special tour and expect one of your visits to last longer than the rest, then it might be a good idea to try to fit in even fewer that day. I think you'll find that you enjoy yourself more at this leisurely pace, and besides: There are no rewards in wine country for making it to the most wineries! Except perhaps the "badge of courage" of an intense 4:00 P.M. hangover.

Taking the Wine Road Less Traveled

If you'd like to visit a winery that's open to visitors only by appointment you'll need to call in advance to set one up. There will usually be a phone number to call on the winery's Web site, and the earlier you call it and make a connection with someone the better. These spots—especially the most popular appointment-only wineries—often book up weeks in advance, which means you'll have the best shot of getting in if you plan ahead.

★See the Appendix for a list of domestic and international wine country tourist offices.

In the Tasting Room

As someone who's been wine tasting many times, I often forget that to the uninitiated it can be a bit puzzling to figure out just what you're supposed to do and how you're supposed to behave on a winery visit. Should you expect to pay for your tastes? Should you spit the wine into those little buckets, or drink it up? Are you supposed to buy something while you're there? And, are you expected to give feedback on the wines, or just smile and sip? Clearly, the experience can be more than just a bit confusing! In order to clear all this up I've outlined some key points you need to know in order to feel comfortable and confident the next time you set foot in a tasting room.

Expect to Pay to Taste

At most wineries open to the public you should expect to pay a smallish fee—usually five to ten dollars—to taste their wines. This will usually get you from three to five one-ounce tastes (roughly equivalent to a half to a full glass altogether). Tasting at smaller wineries or those in lesser-known areas may be less.

Consider Spitting—Seriously

If you're not used to drinking three glasses of wine during the middle of the day, it's a good idea to consider spitting out at least some of the wine you taste during your visits. Besides, swallowing the stuff does little to heighten your tasting experience; in fact, swallow enough wine and you won't be able to enjoy any of it. So, use the spittoons!

Don't Be Afraid to Ask Questions

Winery staffers are there to answer any questions you may have about the spot's wines, its history, and its winemaking philosophy. In fact, asking questions in tasting rooms can be a great way to get more out of your wine country experience. Giving feedback on the wines and your experience is also appreciated, but it's certainly not necessary. And, as with anything, tact is always appropriate.

Don't Feel Obligated to Make a Purchase

If you've paid for your tastes and decide you don't absolutely have to score a bottle of the spot's signature blend, then skip it. You've done your duty by paying to taste, and can feel good about leaving empty-handed. The only caveat I'll throw out is that if you've had special treatment, such as an extended tour, it can be a sign of respect and thanks to make at least a small purchase. And in the rare instance you've been treated to a particularly nice free tasting (lucky you!), this is also a good time to consider making a reasonable purchase as a sign of gratitude. In both instances it's the gesture (not the expenditure!) that counts.

Drink Water

Perhaps this goes without saying, but it's a good idea to balance out all that alcohol intake with water. Not only will water help you get through the day, it'll also come in handy when you're heading out to dinner circa 7:00 P.M. and you don't have a raging hangover.

Buying Wine on the Cheap(er)

Tasting room fees at wineries can often be credited toward purchases you make during your visit, including wine. So, if you're already paying ten dollars to taste a spot's wines, check and see how much bottles for sale there cost. If you're already hankering for a thirty-dollar bottle of Pinot, it may make a lot more sense to shell out the additional twenty dollars and take it home with you to enjoy later.

Where and When to Go

Most wineries that are open to the general public (i.e., as opposed to not at all or by special appointment only) will state so clearly on a sign along the road or just outside their facility. Again, many tourism offices and, increasingly, Web sites devoted to promoting specific wine regions have created maps that point out wineries open to the public along popular wine travel routes. These maps can be indispensable when it comes to planning your trip, as they also make it easy to choose several wineries close to each other that make for convenient tasting room hopping. Most wineries are open daily from midmorning until just about 4:00 P.M., making wine country travel extremely conducive to sleeping in and heading in early as well.

Another thing worth considering is the time of year you choose to do your traveling. Generally, visitors traveling during off-peak times (which include early spring, late fall, and winter) will be rewarded with fewer crowds, more personal attention at wineries, and lower hotel room rates. The only time of year I'd recommend steering clear of is harvest time (around these parts that's from late summer to early fall), when wine country erupts in activity as vintners anxiously haul in their grapes and wineries run at full tilt processing the soon-to-be-fermenting juice. Although this time of year is exciting in wine country, you may find it tinged with a note of frenetic energy that's a bit contrary to relaxation. And this is definitely *not* the time to go if you entertain hopes of meeting winemakers!

Buying Wine on the Road

Visiting wine country may understandably lead you to contemplate bringing some bottles home. It's important to keep a few things in mind when considering buying wine in wine country—namely, how you'll get the good stuff home. If you're fortunate enough to have driven, then taking several bottles or even several cases of wine home is a no-brainer. If, on the other hand, you've flown for your travels, then getting even a few bottles of wine home presents a significantly greater challenge.

While many wineries can ship wine directly to customers through the mail these days (therefore alleviating the need for folks to schlep it home in their suitcases), many still cannot. Again, this boils down to where the winery is located, where recipients reside, and the rules regarding wine shipments that pertain to their respective states. So check to make sure you're eligible to receive wine in the mail. If you're not eligible, you'll need to take it home with you on the plane—so choose your purchases wisely.

Call Ahead for the Best Perks

Particularly at medium- and smaller-sized wineries, calling ahead and announcing your visit can result in some fun additional perks while you're there. These might include meeting an owner or the winemaker him- or herself, taking a tour of the facility, or tasting reserve wines not on the regular tasting room menu. Remember: Wineries are hospitality businesses, and it pays for them to make a lasting impression on guests. If a winery goes out of its way to make your visit special, be sure to thank the staff.

Après Tasting: Stay, Dine, and Play

Taking a little extra time to research attractions in the area where you'll be staying can be highly rewarding. Things to watch for are acclaimed restaurants, festivals, art galleries or exhibits, spa treatments, and outdoor activities like golfing and biking. Tapping into some of these extras can lend another dimension to your understanding of a region while adding to your overall enjoyment of the place. After all, wine is wonderful, but it sure is nice to try something different after spending six hours on the tasting trail! To find out what's going on in an area you're visiting, consult Web sites covering the area, the local tourist board, or the manager or concierge at your hotel.

Quick Tip. Tasting room staffers are also great resources when it comes to tapping into the local events scene. So next time you're tasting, ask away!

Three Ways to Save in Wine Country

Buy a Passport or Festival Pass

Many wine regions host special weekends or festivals during which they sell weekend "passports" that give visitors entry to unlimited wineries for a flat fee. Fees usually represent a significant discount off what you'd otherwise pay to taste on a full weekend of tasting, and passes are sometimes good for hotel and dining discounts as well. Check the list in the Appendix for a roster of annual festivals and passport weekends stateside.

Pack a Picnic Lunch

It being tourist country, wine country can get expensive! A great way to save money is to buy and pack your own picnic lunch each day. You usually don't have to look far to find a gourmet grocer in wine country, and a well-selected sandwich and accoutrements from such a spot are often at least as good as if not better than what you might find in a restaurant! Plus, many wineries allow picnicking on their grounds, and some even have picnic tables set up for this very reason.

Go During the Off Season

Visiting wine country in winter is the best way to save on lodging, and it's also when you'll get the most face time from winery staff. This is when hotels offer deep discounts and special incentives (free massage, anyone?) to coax visitors to wine country. But early spring and late fall are my favorite off seasons, since the weather is better but the crowds are still at bay and the deals still solid.

So Many Wine Regions, So Little Time!

There are tons of fabulous wine regions around the globe just begging for you to visit. Some of the more glamorous include tons of spots in France, Spain, Italy, Portugal, Greece, Canada, South Africa, New Zealand, Tasmania, Argentina, Chile, and Mexico's Baja California. And stateside, you can of course find wine in California, Oregon, Washington State, and New York, but you might also consider visiting the emerging wine regions in spots like Michigan, Virginia, Iowa, and Idaho.

In order to help you sift through all these options and prioritize, I'd like to suggest that you kick off your travels by visiting regions producing the wines that you love most. This will add tremendously to your enjoyment of them when you get back *and* gives you a personal connection with the places you're visiting. There you'll see the lay of the land, meet the people who make it all happen, savor the food, and, most important, drink more of the wines you already enjoy so much. Because all of these things make up what goes into a bottle of wine, there's nothing better than experiencing it firsthand.

Bon voyage!

Acknowledgments

I know it sounds clichéd to say this, but I'll say it anyway because it's absolutely true: Writing a book is hard work! Much harder work, in fact, than I had anticipated back when the excitement of "the deal" was still fresh and the manuscript unwritten. Now that I've crossed the finish line, I'd like to thank a handful of people who helped me get here.

First, I'd like to thank my editor, Lucia Watson, for her enthusiasm for *Hip Tastes* and—perhaps more important—for wine in general. Lucia's sincere interest in the subject and belief in my vision made for a wonderful partnership in bringing the book to life. Lucia, you rock. I'd also like to thank the rest of the team at Viking Studio for their support, flexibility, and dedication to getting the book made. I am particularly grateful to production editor Bruce Giffords, whose keen eye saved me from myself time and again, and to Kate Stark, whose dynamite suggestions and energy in the marketing realm are tremendously appreciated.

Many thanks go to my fabulous agent, Elisabeth Weed, who took a chance on me and helped me hone the proposal that became this book. I'd also like to give a shout-out to my first wine teacher, Mark Davidson, for initially stoking my enthusiasm for the good stuff with his down-to-earth teaching style and funny anecdotes. As well, I am indebted to the charming Robin Kelly O'Connor, president of the Society of Wine Educators, whose frank insights into the manuscript I found invaluable. Robin, I don't know where I'd be without our three-hour "working" lunches, discussing the book!

And last, but most definitely not least, I'd like to thank my parents for steadfastedly believing in my business and creative endeavors, even when they weren't entirely sure what I was working toward. As far as they knew, I was reaching for my dreams, and that was reason enough for their support. Much love, 'rents.

Wines Named for Places
Making Sense of Selected European Wine Place-Names

Wine	Country	Grapes Used
Barbaresco	Italy	Nebbiolo
Barolo	Italy	Nebbiolo
Beaujolais	France	Gamay
Bordeaux	France	**Whites:** Sémillon, Sauvignon Blanc **Reds:** Cabernet Sauvignon, Merlot, Cabernet Franc, Petit Verdot, Malbec
Brunello di Montalcino	Italy	Sangiovese (Brunello clone, a.k.a. Sangiovese Grosso)

Wine	Country	Grapes Used
Burgundy	France	**Whites:** Chardonnay **Reds:** Pinot Noir
Cava	Spain	Xarel-lo, Parellada, Macabeo, Chardonnay
Chablis	France	Chardonnay
Champagne	France	Chardonnay, Pinot Noir, Pinot Meunier
Châteauneuf-du-Pape	France	Grenache, Syrah, Cinsault, Mourvèdre, and more
Chianti	Italy	Sangiovese and more
Côtes-du-Rhône	France	Grenache, Cinsault, Mourvèdre, and more
Hermitage	France	Syrah
Navarra	Spain	**Whites:** Viura, Chardonnay **Reds:** Grenache, Tempranillo, Cabernet Sauvignon, Merlot, and more
Port	Portugal	Tinta Barroca, Touriga Nacional, Touriga Francesa, Tinta Roriz, Tinta Cão, and more
Priorat	Spain	Cabernet Sauvignon, Carignan, Grenache, Merlot, Mourvèdre, and more

Wine	Country	Grapes Used
Rioja	Spain	**Whites:** Viura, Malvasia **Reds:** Tempranillo, Grenache, Graciano, Mazuelo
Sancerre	France	Sauvignon Blanc
Sauternes	France	Sémillon, Sauvignon Blanc
Sherry	Spain	Palomino, Pedro Ximénez, Muscat of Alexandria
Tokay (a.k.a. Tokaji)	Hungary	Furmint, Hárslevelü, Muscat Blanc à Petits Grains
Valpolicella	Italy	Corvina, Molinara, Rondinella
Vouvray	France	Chenin Blanc

Phonetic Guide to Wine Terms
How to Pronounce Common Wine Words

Term	Pronunciation
Albariño	al-bar-EEN-yoh
Alsace	al-ZOSS
Alto Adige	altoh ADD-eeghay
Amontillado	ah-mohn-tee-AH-doh
Auslese	owsh-LAY-zuh
Banyuls	ban-yools
Barsac	bar-zahck

Term	Pronunciation
Beaujolais	bow-jhowe-lay
Beerenauslese	bear-ehn-owsh-LAY-zuh
blanc de blancs	blahnc duh blahnc
blanc de noirs	blahnc duh nwahr
Bordeaux	bore-doh
Botrytis	buh-TRY-tiss
Bourgogne	boor-GUHN-yuh
Brouilly	broo-wee
Brunello di Montalcino	broon-EL-oh dee MOAN-tal-CHEE-no
brut	brute
Cabernet Sauvignon	cab-er-nay SOH-veen-yon
Carmenère	carmen-air
Chablis	shab-LEE
Champagne	sham-pain
Chardonnay	shar-dohn-AY
Chassagne-Montrachet	shass-on-yuh moan-rah-shay
Châteauneuf-du-Pape	shah-tow-NOOF doo pop
Chénas	SHAY-noss
Chenin Blanc	shen-in blahnc
Chevalier-Montrachet	sheh-vall-yay moan-rah-shay
Chianti	key-ON-tee
Chinon	SHEE-non
Condrieu	con-dree-uhr
Corton-Charlemagne	core-TONE shar-luh-mane

Term	Pronunciation
Côte de Beaune	coat duh bone
Crémant	CRAY-mohnt
crianza	cree-ON-zuh
cru	crew
cuvée	koo-VAY
Dolcetto	dole-CHET-toh
domaine	doh-men
Eiswein	EYES-vine
Fleurie	fluh-ree
frizzante	frizz-AUN-tay
Fumé Blanc	FOOM-ay blahnc
Gewürztraminer	guh-VERTZ-tra-min-er
Gigondas	jhee-gohn-doss
grand cru	grahn crew
Grüner Veltliner	groo-ner velt-leen-er
Halbtrocken	halb-trohk-en
Hermitage	hair-mee-tahj
Kabinett	cab-in-ett
Languedoc-Roussillon	long-gwah-dock roo-SEE-ohn
lieu-dit	lee-uhr dee
liqueur	li-kyer
Loire	low-wahr
Madeira	mad-air-uh
Malvasia	mal-vay-zee-uh
Manzanilla	man-thuh-NEE-yuh
Margaux	mar-goh
Mercurey	mair-cure-ay

Term	Pronunciation
Merlot	mer-LOW
Meursault	MAIR-sow
Monthélie	moan-TAY-lee
Montrachet	moan-rah-shay
Morgon	more-GOHN
Moscato	mow-SKA-toe
Mosel-Saar-Ruwer	MOW-zell sahr roo-ver
Moulin-à-Vent	moo-len ah vahn
Müller-Thurgau	MEW-luhr TER-gow
Muscadet	MOO-skah-day
Muscat	moos-ka
Navarra	nuh-VAHR-uh
Nebbiolo	neb-EE-oh-loh
oloroso	oh-lo-ROH-so
Pauillac	POY-yak
Penedès	pen-eh-DETH
Pernand-Vergelesses	pear-nahn vair-GHEL-ess
Pessac-Léognan	pess-ak LAY-ohn-yon
Petite Sirah	puh-TEET sir-ah
Petit Verdot	puh-tee vair-DOH
Pfalz	falls
Pinotage	pee-noh-TAHJ
Pinot Grigio	PEE-noh GREE-ghi-oh
Pinot Meunier	PEE-noh muhn-YAY
Pinot Noir	PEE-noh nwahr
Pouilly-Fuissé	PWEE-yee foo-wee-SAY
Pouilly-Fumé	PWEE-yee foo-MAY
premier cru	prem-ee-YAY crew

Term	Pronunciation
Priorat	PREE-or-aht
Prosecco	prow-SECK-oh
Puligny-Montrachet	poo-leen-yee moan-rah-shay
Recioto	re-chee-OWE-tow
Rheingau	RINE-gow
Rias Baixas	REE-us BYE-shuss
Riesling	REESE-leen
Rioja	ree-OH-hah
riserva	ree-ZERV-ah
Roussanne	ROO-sahn
Sancerre	sohn-sair
Sangiovese	san-gee-oh-VAY-say
Sauternes	SOH-tairn
Sauvignon Blanc	SOH-veen-yohn blahnc
Savennières	sah-vehn-YAIR
sec	seck
Sémillon	SAY-mee-yohn
Soave	soh-AH-vay
sommelier	soh-mel-YAY
Spätlese	SCHPATE-lay-zuh
Spumante	spoo-MON-tee
St.-Aubin	sant-oh-ban
St.-Émilion	san-TAY-mee-lyohn
St.-Estèphe	san-tes-TEFF
St.-Julien	san-joo-lee-en
Tempranillo	tem-prah-NEE-yoh
terroir	tehr-WAHR
Tokay	toke-EYE

Term	Pronunciation
Trocken	trohk-en
Valpolicella	val-pole-ee-CHEL-uh
vendange tardive	von-donj tar-deeve
Verdejo	vair-DAY-yoh
Verdicchio	vair-DEE-kee-yoh
Vinho Verde	veen-oh VAIR-day
vins doux naturels	van doo NAH-ture-el
Viognier	VEE-ohn-yay
Vosne-Romanée	von roman-ay
Vouvray	VOOV-ray

Region, Producer, and Vintage Guide
Road Map of Regions, Including Quality and Value Designations

Region	Well-Known Subregions	Recommended Producers★	Recent Top Vintages
ARGENTINA			
Mendoza	Luján, Maipú, San Martin	Catena Zapata, Lurton, Norton, San Telmo, Susana Balbo, Weinert **Value:** Etchart, Mariposa, Paul Hobbs, Peña-flor, Santa Ana, Trapiche	1999, 2002, 2003, 2005

★ "Domaine," "Château," and similar terms have been omitted from the names of properties where applicable.

Region	Well-Known Subregions	Recommended Producers	Recent Top Vintages
AUSTRALIA			
Southern Australia	Adelaide Hills, Barossa Valley, Clare Valley, Coonawarra, Eden Valley, Hunter Valley, Langhorne Creek, McLaren Vale, Padthaway, Riverland, Victoria	Chapel Hill, d'Arenberg, Elderton, Henschke, Katnook, Mountadam, Penfolds, Petaluma, Peter Lehmann, Reynella, Seaview, Wolf Blass, Wynns **Value:** Andrew Garrett, Coriole, Elderton, Hardys, Layer Cake, Leasingham, Turkey Flat, Yalumba	1998, 2001, 2003, 2004, 2005
Western Australia	Great Southern, Margaret River, Pemberton, Swan Valley	Cape Clairault, Cape Mentelle, Evans & Tate, Leeuwin Estate, Moss Wood, Pierro, Plantagenet, Vasse Felix **Value:** Goundrey, Karrivale	1998, 2001, 2002, 2005

Region	Well-Known Subregions	Recommended Producers	Recent Top Vintages
AUSTRIA			
	Burgenland, Kamptal, Kremstal, Wachau	Giesselmann, Hiedler, Hirsch, Jurtschitsch Sonnhof, Nikolaihof, Prager, Schloss Gobelsburg, Willi Opitz **Value:** Bründlmayer	1995, 1997, 1999, 2003, 2004
CHILE			
Acon-cagua and Central Valley	Aconcagua Valley, Casablanca Valley, Curicó Valley, Maipo Valley, Maule Valley, Rapel Valley	Caliterra, Concha y Toro, Erra-zuriz, Casa Lapostolle, Montes, Terra Noble, Torres, Valdivieso, Villard, Vina Casablanca **Value:** Los Boldos, Canepa, Luis Felipe Edwards, Viña de la Rosa, Santa Carolina	1999, 2001, 2003, 2005

Region	Well-Known Subregions	Recommended Producers	Recent Top Vintages
FRANCE			
Alsace	**Grand crus (selected):** Eichberg, Frank-stein, Froehn, Hengst, Rangen, Schlossberg, Schoenenbourg	Hugel, J. Becker, Marcel Deiss, Paul Ginglinger, Pierre Sparr, Trimbach, Weinbach, Zind-Humbrecht **Value:** Charles Baur, J. Hauller & Fils	1990, 1994, 1998, 2000, 2001, 2002, 2004, 2005
Beaujolais	Beaujolais-Villages, Brouilly, Chénas, Côte de Brouilly, Fleurie, Morgon, Moulin-à-Vent	Georges Duboeuf, des Jacques, La-fond, Thivin, Vincent et Fils **Value:** Lucky you—it's pretty much all good value!	1999, 2000, 2003, 2005
Bordeaux, Left Bank	Barsac (sweet), Margaux, Pauillac, Pessac-Léognan, St.-Estèphe, St.-Julien, Sauternes (sweet) **Value:** Cérons (sweet), Bor-deaux Supérieur, Moulis-en-Médoc	**First growths (1855 classifi-cation):** Haut-Brion, Lafite Roth-schild, Latour, Margaux, Mou-ton Rothschild	1982, 1986, 1989, 1990, 1995, 1996, 2000, 2003, 2005

Region	Well-Known Subregions	Recommended Producers	Recent Top Vintages
		Other recommended producers: Au Baron de Pichon-Longueville, Carbonnieux, Calon-Ségur, Cos d'Estournel, Gruaud-Larose, Lagrange, Lascombes, Léoville-Barton, Lynch-Bages, La Mission Haut-Brion, Montrose, Palmer, Pichon Longueville Comtesse de Lalande, Rieussec (sweet), Suduiraut (sweet), La Tour-Haut-Brion, d'Yquem (sweet)	

Region	Well-Known Subregions	Recommended Producers	Recent Top Vintages
		Value: Branaire-Ducru, Camensac, Chasse-Spleen, Doisy-Védrines (sweet), de Fieuzal, Haut-Bages-Libéral, Haut-Marbuzet, Kirwan, Phélan-Ségur, Poujeaux, Sénéjac, Smith-Haut-Lafitte	
Bordeaux, Right Bank	Pomerol, St.-Émilion **Value:** Blaye, Bourg, Canon-Fronsac, Côtes-Canon-Fronsac, Premières Côtes de Blaye	Angélus, Ausone, Belair, Cheval Blanc, La Conseillante, Figeac, Pavie, Petit-Village, Pétrus, Le Pin, Trotanoy, Vieux Château Certan **Value:** Beau-regard, Le Bon Pasteur, de Bousquet, Canon-Moueix, Cassagne-Haut-Canon, Clos René, Crusquet-de-Lagarcie, La Dominique,	1982, 1986, 1989, 1990, 1995, 1998, 2000, 2003, 2005

Region	Well-Known Subregions	Recommended Producers	Recent Top Vintages
		Le Gay, Grand Mayne, Haut-Guiraud, Laroze, Magdelaine, Menaudat, Moulinet, Plince, Rouget, de Sales, Segonzac, La Tour Figeac	
Burgundy, whites	Bâtard-Montrachet, Chassagne-Montrachet, Chevalier-Montrachet, Corton, Corton-Charlemagne, Meursault, Montrachet, Puligny-Montrachet **Value:** Beaune Premier Cru, Pernand-Vergelesses, Pouilly-Fuissé, St.-Aubin, St.-Véran	Arnoux Père & Fils, Bouchard Père & Fils, Étienne Sauzet, Faiveley, Georges Deléger, Guy Roulot, Jean-Marc Boillot, Joseph Drouhin, Leflaive, Louis Jadot, Louis Latour, Marius Delarche, Michelot, Pierre Morey, Ramonet, de la Romanée-Conti **Value:** Auvigne, Georges Duboeuf, Guffens-Heynen, Jean-Claude Bachelet, Louis Jadot, Olivier Leflaive, Marc Colin, Vincent et Fils	1986, 1989, 1995, 1996, 2000, 2002, 2004, 2005

Region	Well-Known Subregions	Recommended Producers	Recent Top Vintages
Burgundy, reds	Bonnes Mares, Chambertin, Clos de la Roche, Corton, Gevrey-Chambertin, Grand Echézeaux, Musigny, Pommard, Richebourg, La Romanée, La Tâche, Volnay, Vosne-Romanée **Value:** Chorey-lès-Beaune, Côte de Beaune-Villages, Côte de Nuits-Villages, Givry, Mercurey, Monthelie, Santenay, Savigny-lès-Beaune	Armand Rousseau, Bouchard Père, et Fils, du Château de Vosne-Romanée, Dujac, Faiveley, Georges Roumier, Hubert de Montille, Jean Tardy, Joseph Drouhin, Joseph Roty, Louis Jadot, Moillard, Mommessin, Mongeard-Mugneret, René Engel, de la Romanée-Conti, Trapet **Value:** Anne Gros, Arnoux Père et Fils, Bernard Bachelet et Fils, des Comtes Lafon, François Raquillet, Leroy, Parent, Tollot-Beaut, Vincent Girardin	1990, 1995, 1996, 1999, 2002, 2003, 2005

Region	Well-Known Subregions	Recommended Producers	Recent Top Vintages
Chablis	**Grand crus:** Blanchot, Bougros, Grenouilles, La Moutonne, Les Preuses, Valmur, Vaudésir **Premier crus (selected):** Côte de Léchet, Fourchaume, Mont de Milieu, Montée de Tonnerre, Montmains, Vaillons	Billaud-Simon, Jean Collet, Jean-Marie Raveneau, Joseph Drouhin, Michel Laroche, René et Vincent Dauvissat, William Fèvre **Value:** La Chablisienne, François Raveneau, Jean-Marc Brocard, Marc Meneau	1986, 1989, 1995, 1996, 2000, 2002, 2005
Loire	Bonnezeaux, Bourgueil, Chinon, Coteaux du Layon Menetou-Salon, Muscadet de Sèvre-et-Maine, Pouilly-Fumé, Quarts-de-Chaume (sweet), Sancerre, Saumur-Champigny, Savennières, St.-Nicolas-de-Bourgueil	Charles Joguet, Christian Thirot, Gitton, Henri Bourgeois, Lucien Crochet, N. Joly, Vincent Pinard, Yannick Amirault **Value:** de Beauregard, Chasiot, Claude Michot, Didier Dagueneau, Henry Pellé	1990, 1996, 2002, 2005

Region	Well-Known Subregions	Recommended Producers	Recent Top Vintages
Northern Rhône	Condrieu (white), Cornas, Côte-Rôtie, Crozes-Hermitage, Hermitage, St.-Joseph	Delas, E. Guigal, François Villard, Jean-Louis Chave, M. Chapoutier, M. Sorrel, Paul Jaboulet Aîné, Pierre Barge, Yves Cuilleron **Value:** Albert Belle, Chave, Georges Vernay, Tain-Hermitage, Tardieu-Laurent	1990, 1995, 1996, 1999, 2003, 2005, 2006
Southern Rhône	Châteauneuf-du-Pape, Côtes-du-Rhône Villages, Gigondas, Vacqueyras	Beaucastel, Clos des Papes, Fortia, Pierre Usseglio, Rayas, Vieux Donjon, Vieux Télégraphe **Value:** les Clos des Cazaux, Montfaucon, Montmirail, Moulin de la Gardette, des Tours, du Trignon	1990, 1995, 1998, 1999, 2000, 2001, 2003, 2004, 2005, 2006

Region	Well-Known Subregions	Recommended Producers	Recent Top Vintages
GERMANY			
Mosel-Saar-Ruwer	**Vineyards (selected):** Bernkasteler Doctor, Lay, Niederberg Helden, Piesporter Goldtröpfchen, Prälat, Schlossberg, Sonnenuhr, Treppchen, Würzgarten	Dr. Loosen, Fritz Haag, J. J. Prüm, Joh. Jos. Christoffel Erben, Selbach-Oster, Willi Schaefer **Value:** Loosen Bros. "Dr. L"	1990, 1999, 2001, 2002, 2003, 2004, 2005
Rheingau	**Vineyards (selected):** Berg Schlossberg, Hohenrain, Mannberg, Marcobrunn, Schloss Johannisberg, Sonnenberg	Bernhard Breuer, Franz Künstler, Jakob Jung, Josef Leitz, Robert Weil, Schloss Schönborn **Value:** Leitz "Dragonstone"	1990, 1999, 2001, 2002, 2003, 2004, 2005
ITALY			
Friuli Venezia Giulia	Collio, Colli Orientali del Friuli, Friuli-Grave	Jermann, Mario Schiopetto **Value:** Plozner	1997, 2003, 2004
Piedmont	Barbaresco, Barbera d'Alba, Barbera d'Asti, Barolo, Gattinara, Gavi, Moscato d'Asti	Gaja, Ceretto, Pio Cesare, Francesco Rinaldi, Vietti **Value:** Bricco Rosso	1989, 1990, 1996, 1997, 1998, 1999, 2000, 2001
Trentino–Alto Adige	Alto Adige, Teroldego Rotaliano, Trentino	Alois Lageder, Josef Hofstätter, Tiefenbrunner **Value:** Niedermayr	1997, 2003, 2004

Region	Well-Known Subregions	Recommended Producers	Recent Top Vintages
Tuscany	Brunello di Montalcino, Chianti, Rosso di Montalcino, Vino Nobile di Montepulciano	Antinori, Biondi-Santi, Brunelli, Conti Costanti, Masseto, Ornellaia, Sassicaia, Solaia, Tignanello **Value:** Cafaggio	1990, 1997, 1999, 2001, 2003
Verona	Soave, Valpolicella	Allegrini, Roberto Anselmi, Giuseppe Quintarelli, Santa Sofia, Tommasi **Value:** Masi	1997, 1998, 2003, 2004
NEW ZEALAND			
North Island	Auckland, Hawkes Bay, Martinborough, Waiheke Island	Craggy Range, Destiny Bay, Dry River, Te Awa Farms, Te Mata **Value:** Oyster Bay, Villa Maria	1998, 2000, 2002, 2004, 2006
South Island	Central Otago, Marlborough, Nelson	Carrick, Cloudy Bay, Isabel, Kim Crawford, Pegasus Bay, Seresin, Spy Valley **Value:** Matua, Oyster Bay	2000, 2002, 2004, 2006

Region	Well-Known Subregions	Recommended Producers	Recent Top Vintages
PORTUGAL			
Douro Valley (port)	Douro	Broadbent, Churchill, Graham, Osborne, Quinta do Noval, Ramos-Pinto, Smith Wood-house, Taylor Fladgate **Value:** Fonseca, Warre	**Vintage port:** 1963, 1970, 1977, 1982, 1985, 1991, 1992, 1994, 1997, 2000, 2003
Madeira		Blandy's, Hen-riques & Henriques, Madeira Wine Company **Value:** Broadbent	1963, 1966, 1970, 1975, 1977, 1983, 1985, 1991, 1997, 2000
Other (table wines)	Bairrada, Dão, Vinho Verde	Quinta da Tamariz, Quinta de Saes, Quinta do Azevedo, Quinta dos Roques **Value:** Duque de Viseu	2000, 2003, 2004, 2005

Region	Well-Known Subregions	Recommended Producers	Recent Top Vintages
SOUTH AFRICA			
	Overberg, Paarl, Stellenbosch, Walker Bay	L'Avenir, Backsberg, Bouchard Finlayson, Delaire, Etienne Fairview, Graham Beck, Kanonkop, Klein Constantia, Meerlust, Le Riche, Rustenberg, Thelema Mountain **Value:** Avontuur, Le Bonheur, Delheim, Fleur du Cap, Nederburg	2000, 2001, 2003, 2005
SPAIN			
Navarra	Ribera Alta, Ribera Baja	Castillo de Monjardín, Julián Chivite, Magaña, Nekeas **Value:** Artazu, Príncipe de Viana, Vinícola Navarra	2001, 2005
Priorat		Clos Erasmus, Clos Mogador, Mas d'En Gil, Vinícola del Priorat **Value:** Alvaro Palacios, Mas Igneus Fa 206	1998, 1999, 2000, 2001, 2002, 2003, 2004

Region	Well-Known Subregions	Recommended Producers	Recent Top Vintages
Ribera del Duero		Alejándro Fernández, Ismael Arroyo, Mauro, Pago de Carraovejas, Pingus, Vega Sicilia **Value:** Alión	1994, 1995, 1996, 2000, 2001, 2003, 2005
Rioja	Rioja Alavesa, Rioja Alta, Rioja Baja	Barón de Ley, Contino, R. López de Heredia Viña Tondonia, Marqués de Riscal, Muga, La Rioja Alta **Value:** Campo Viejo, Marqués de Cáceres, Marqués de Griñón	1994, 1995, 2001, 2005
UNITED STATES			
California, North Coast: Mendocino		Ceago Vinegarden, Esterlina, Husch, Mendocino Farms, Navarro, Patianna Organic Vineyards, Roederer Estate (sparkling), Scharffenberger (sparkling) **Value:** Fetzer, Graziano	2001, 2002, 2004

Region	Well-Known Subregions	Recommended Producers	Recent Top Vintages
California, North Coast: Napa	Atlas Peak, Carneros, Howell Mountain, Mount Veeder, Oak Knoll, Oakville, Rutherford, Spring Mountain, Stag's Leap	Araujo, Atlas Peak, Blackbird, Buoncristiani, Cain, Cakebread, Caymus, Chateau Montelena, Corison, Diamond Creek, Domaine Chandon (sparkling), Etude, Honig, Opus One, Pride, Rombauer, Smith-Madrone, Staglin, Swanson, Turley **Value:** Beringer, Hess Select, Mumm Napa (sparkling)	1990, 1991, 1992, 1994, 1995, 1996, 1997, 1999, 2001, 2002, 2004

Region	Well-Known Subregions	Recommended Producers	Recent Top Vintages
California, North Coast: Sonoma	Alexander Valley, Carneros, Chalk Hill, Dry Creek Valley, Russian River Valley, Sonoma Coast, Sonoma Valley	Arrowood, Chalk Hill Winery, Cline, De Loach, Flowers, Gary Farrell, Gundlach-Bundschu, Hobo Wine Company, Iron Horse (sparkling), Kistler, Kunde, Landmark, Lava Vine, Ledson, Medlock Ames, Michel-Schlumberger, Ravenswood, Roshambo, Williams Selyem **Value:** Benziger, Chateau Souverain, Clos du Bois, Sonoma-Cutrer	1990, 1992, 1994, 1995, 2001, 2002, 2004

| California, Central Coast | Carmel Valley, Livermore Valley, Monterey, Santa Cruz Mountains, Santa Lucia Highlands | Ahlgren, Banyan, Beauregard, Bernardus, Bonny Doon, Burrell School, Calera, Chalone, Cinnabar, David Bruce, Hunter Hill, Kathryn Kennedy, Mount Eden Vineyards, Organic Wine Works, Pisoni, Ridge

Value: Michael David, Morgan, Wente | 1997, 1999, 2002, 2003, 2004 |
| California, South Central Coast | Arroyo Grande, Edna Valley, Paso Robles, Santa Maria Valley, Santa Rita Hills, Santa Ynez Valley | Au Bon Climat, Babcock, Beckmen, Brewer-Clifton, Domaine Alfred, Fiddle-head, Flying Goat Cellars, Foxen, Hartley Ostini Hitch-ing Post, Melville, Qupé, Rancho Sisquoc, Sea Smoke, Wild Horse, Zaca Mesa

Value: Byron, Edna Valley Vineyard, Santa Barbara Winery | 1997, 1999, 2002, 2003, 2004 |

New York	Finger Lakes, The Hamptons, Hudson River, Lake Erie, North Fork of Long Island	Fox Run, Glenora, Hargrave, Lamoreaux Landing, Millbrook, Pellegrini, Treleaven, Wagner **Value:** Rivendell	2005
Oregon	Columbia Valley, Rogue Valley, Walla Walla Valley, Willamette Valley	Adelsheim, Amity, Archery Summit, Beaux Frères, Benton-Lane, Chehalem, Domaine Drouhin, Domaine Serene, Eyrie Vineyards, Ponzi, Rex Hill, Sokol Blosser **Value:** A to Z, Bethel Heights	1992, 1994, 1998, 1999, 2001, 2002, 2004, 2005
Washington State	Columbia Valley, Walla Walla Valley, Yakima Valley	Andrew Will, Covey Run, De Lille, Hogue, Kiona, L'École No. 41, Leonetti, Quilceda Creek, Washington Hills **Value:** Chateau Ste. Michelle, Columbia Crest	1992, 1994, 1998, 2000, 2001, 2003, 2005, 2006

U.S. Retailers
Recommended Bricks-and-Mortar
and Online Merchants

Visit winezap.com, wineaccess.com, and wine-searcher.com for
wines available at merchants across the country.

Acker, Merrall & Condit
Location: New York, NY
Tel.: 212-787-1700
Web: ackerstore.com

Astor Wines & Spirits
Location: New York, NY
Tel.: 212-674-7500
Web: astorwines.com

Beverages & More
Location: various, CA
Tel.: 877-77-BEVMO
Web: bevmo.com

Burgundy Wine Company
Location: New York, NY
Tel.: 888-898-8448
Web: burgundywinecompany.com

Costco
Location: various, nationwide
Tel.: 800-774-2678
Web: costco.com

Crush Wine & Spirits
Location: New York, NY
Tel.: 212-980-WINE
Web: crushwineco.com

Ferry Plaza Wine Merchant
Location: San Francisco, CA
Tel.: 415-391-9400
Web: fpwm.com

Hi-Time Wine Cellars
Location: Costa Mesa, CA
Tel.: 800-331-3005
Web: hitimewine.net

Italian Wine Merchants
Location: New York, NY
Tel.: 212-473-2323
Web: italianwinemerchantstore.com

K&L Wine Merchants
Location: San Francisco and Hollywood, CA
Tel.: 877-KLWines
Web: klwines.com

Kermit Lynch Wine Merchant
Location: Berkeley, CA
Tel.: 510-524-1524
Web: kermitlynch.com

Morrell & Co.
Location: New York, NY
Tel.: 212-688-9370
Web: morrellwine.com

North Berkeley Wine Imports
Location: Berkeley, CA
Tel.: 888-266-6585
Web: northberkeleyimports.com

Sam's Wine & Spirits
Location: Chicago, IL
Tel.: 800-777-9137
Web: samswine.com

Sherry-Lehmann Wine & Spirits Merchants
Location: New York, NY
Tel.: 212-838-7500
Web: sherry-lehmann.com

67 Wines & Spirits
Location: New York, NY
Tel.: 212-724-6767
Web: 67wine.com

Twenty-Twenty Wine Merchants
Location: Los Angeles, CA
Tel.: 310-447-2020
Web: 2020wines.com

Wally's
Location: Los Angeles, CA
Tel.: 888-9-WALLYS
Web: wallywine.com

Wine Cask
Location: Santa Barbara, CA
Tel:. 805-966-9463
Web: winecask.com

The Wine Club
Location: various, CA
Tel.: 800-966-5432
Web: thewineclub.com

The Wine House
Location: Los Angeles, CA
Tel.: 866-922-9471
Web: winehouse.com

Zachys
Location: Scarsdale, NY
Tel.: 866-922-9471
Web: zachys.com

Wine Festivals and Local Events
Recurring Wine Events Found Throughout the United States

Consult localwineevents.com for regularly updated local listings.

Spring
Dallas Wine and Food Festival, Dallas, TX
Food & Wine Magazine Classic, Aspen, CO
Golden Glass, San Francisco, CA
The Grand Wine and Food Affair, Houston, TX
Hospice du Rhône, Paso Robles, CA
Paso Robles Wine Festival, Paso Robles, CA

Portland Indie Wine Festival, Portland, OR
Rhone Rangers, San Francisco, CA
Santa Cruz Mountains Winegrowers Passport Weekend,
    Santa Cruz, CA
Scottsdale Culinary Festival, Scottsdale, AZ
Sonoma Valley Film Festival, Sonoma County, CA
Taste of Washington, Seattle, WA
Wine and Food Experience, New Orleans, LA
Wine Fest, Ann Arbor, MI
World of Pinot Noir, Shell Beach, CA
ZinFest, Lodi, CA

Summer
Auction Napa Valley, Napa County, CA
Central Coast Wine Classic, Shell Beach, CA
Culinary Arts Festival, Telluride, CO
Finger Lakes Wine Festival, Watkins Glen, NY
Home Winemakers Classic, Napa County, CA
International Pinot Noir Celebration, McMinnville, OR
International Wine and Food Festival, Washington, DC
New Mexico Wine Festival, Bernalillo, NM
Pinot Noir Festival, San Francisco, CA
Santa Barbara Wine Festival, Santa Barbara, CA
Showcase of Wine and Food, Sonoma County, CA
Sun Valley Food and Wine Festival, Sun Valley, ID
Temecula Valley Balloon & Wine Festival, Temecula, CA
Wine and Food Festival, Key West, FL

Fall
Autumn Food and Wine Festival, Lake Tahoe, NV
Chicago Wine & Food Festival, Chicago, IL
Denver International Wine Festival, Denver, CO
Detroit Uncorked, Detroit, MI
Hudson Valley Wine & Food Fest, Red Hook, NY
Los Angeles Wine Fest, Hollywood, CA
Miami International Wine Fair, Miami, FL
San Antonio New World Wine & Food Festival, San Antonio,
    TX
San Diego Bay Wine & Food Festival, San Diego, CA
Savor the Season, Los Angeles, CA
Sonoma County Harvest Fair, Santa Posa, CA
St. Louis Wine Festival, St. Louis, MO
Wine & Chile Fiesta, Santa Fe, NM
Wine South, Atlanta, GA

Winter
Atlanta Fine Wine Festival, Atlanta, GA
Boston Wine Expo, Boston, MA
Cincinnati International Wine Festival, Cincinnati, OH
Harvest Wine Celebration, Temecula, CA
International Festival of Wines and Food, Columbia, SC
Masters of Food & Wine, Carmel, CA
Naples Winter Wine Festival, Naples, FL
Russian River Wine Trail, Sonoma County, CA
South Beach Wine & Food Festival, South Beach, FL
Southwest Michigan Wine Trail, Lake Michigan Shore, MN
Twin Cities Food & Wine Experience, Minneapolis, MN
Vintners' Holidays, Yosemite National Park, CA
Zinfandel Advocates & Producers ("ZAP"), San Francisco, CA

Wine Tourism Resources
Resources for Domestic and Global Wine Travel

Argentina/Mendoza Office of Tourism
descubramendoza.com

Australian Wine Bureau
wineaustralia.com

Bordeaux Office of Tourism
bordeaux-tourisme.com

Burgundy Regional Tourism Council
burgundy-tourism.com

Chilean Tourism Promotion Corporation
visit-chile.org

Finger Lakes Tourism Alliance (New York)
fingerlakes.org

French Tourist Office
francetourism.com

Wines of Germany
germanwineusa.org

Italian Government Tourist Board
italiantourism.com

Napa Valley Conference & Visitors Bureau
napavalley.org

New Zealand Wine
nzwine.com

Oregon Wine
oregonwine.org

Portuguese Trade Bureau
portugal.org

Santa Cruz Mountains Winegrowers Association
scmwa.com

Sonoma Valley Visitors Bureau
sonomavalley.com

South African Tourism Bureau
southafrica.net

Spanish Tourism Bureau
spain.info

Uncork New York!
newyorkwines.org

Washington Wine Commission
washingtonwine.org

Wine Schools, Classes, and Helpful Resources
Taking It Further

American Court of Master Sommeliers
mastersommeliers.org

American Institute of Wine & Food
aiwf.org

American Wine Society
americanwinesociety.org

Chicago Wine School
wineschool.com

Copia: The American Center for Wine, Food & the Arts
copia.org

Culinary Institute of America
ciachef.edu

Hip Tastes
hiptastes.com

Institute of Masters of Wine
masters-of-wine.org

International Sommelier Guild
internationalsommelier.com

Learn About Wine
learnaboutwine.com

Les Dames d'Escoffier
ldei.org

Society of Wine Educators
societyofwineeducators.org

The Wine Institute
wineinstitute.org

Index